The Princely Chandos: A Memoir Of James Brydges, Afterwards The First Duke Of Chandos

John Robert Robinson

THE

PRINCELY CHANDOS

A Memoir

OF

JAMES BRYDGES

PAYMASTER-GENERAL TO THE FORCES ABROAD DURING THE MOST BRILLIANT PART OF THE DUKE OF MARLBOROUGH'S MILITARY CAREER, 1705—1711

AFTERWARDS

THE FIRST DUKE OF CHANDOS

BY

JOHN ROBERT ROBINSON

"At Timon's villa let us pass a day."
ALEXANDER POPE.

ILLUSTRATED

LONDON
SAMPSON LOW, MARSTON & COMPANY
Limited
St. Dunstan's House
FETTER LANE, FLEET STREET, E.C.
1893

JKD

James Brydges.
First Duke of Chandos.

PREFACE.

AMONG the many remarkable personages of the time of Queen Anne and the early Georgian period, James Brydges, the first Duke of Chandos, is conspicuous.

His almost regal style of living, and his magnanimous conduct, induced the people of those times to add to the ducal style the prefix " Grand," and subsequently " Princely "; hence the title of this volume. Questions respecting the Duke of Chandos and his palace of Canons frequently occur in literary and other periodicals, no doubt because there has hitherto been no authentic record of his career.

While the Duke of Chandos, then Mr. Brydges, still held the post of Paymaster to

the Forces abroad, an inquiry into the accounts of
that and other Government offices was instituted
by Parliament. The Duke was fortunate enough
to escape direct censure at the hands of the
Commons; but it is certain that the foundation
of his fortune was laid during his tenure of
that office.

Upon vacating the office of Paymaster, and
inheriting the family title and estates, Lord
Chandos found leisure to erect the magnificent
palace and lay out the grounds of Canons—
destined hardly to outlast the life of their owner.

Much curiosity still exists respecting the
edifice and its surroundings, no picture, print, or
drawing representing Canons as a whole being
known. Nor has any description hitherto
appeared in print that will help to reproduce
the once famous building and grounds. The
author trusts he has accomplished this task in
the following pages.

Attention is directed to the fact, that in the
numerous works which treat of the military

career of the Duke of Marlborough no allusion
is made to the friendship that appears (by their
correspondence) to have existed between the
Duke and Mr. Brydges, then his Paymaster.

Upon the wane of the Duke of Chandos'
fortunes there were not wanting some who took
the opportunity of misrepresenting his purposes
and professions, and this the public resented in
one notorious instance—that of Pope. The
Duke's generous and magnanimous disposition
stood him in good stead when deserted by the
fickle goddess, Fortune. It is to be regretted,
however, that at this period an erroneous rumour
concerning the birth and social position of the
Duke's third wife gained credence which has been
handed down to the present day. The author has
finally disposed of an injurious popular error.

He has endeavoured to place before the public
a work not only historically accurate and of use for
reference, but generally entertaining, on a subject
hitherto treated in short articles in biographical
works, and these in many instances untrustworthy.

The author begs to acknowledge the courteous
replies which he has received to the communi-
cations addressed to many persons in the course
of his investigations.   Also for the assistance
received in the course of his work from Mr.
H. H. Robinson, whom he has also to thank for
aid in selecting the illustrations.

LONDON, *Feb.*, 1893.

CONTENTS.

CHAPTER I.

CHAPTER II.

CHAPTER III.

CHAPTER IV.

CHAPTER XIII.

CHAPTER XIV.

CHAPTER XV.

CHAPTER XVI.

CHAPTER XVII.

CHAPTER XXI.

LIST OF ILLUSTRATIONS.

THE PRINCELY CHANDOS.

CHAPTER I.

Genealogy of the Brydges family—Birth of James Brydges—
Early youth—Enters New College, Oxford, as a Fellow
Commoner — Returned as Member of Parliament for
Hereford, 1698—Deputed by the Commons in 1701 to
carry up to the Lords impeachment against Lord Halifax
—Moves motion in the House of Commons purporting
to attack Lord Somers—Appointed one of the Commis-
sioners to inquire into the state of the Public Accounts,
1703 — An example of Mr. Brydges' assiduity—Ap-
pointed Paymaster-General of the Forces abroad—Con-
gratulatory letter from the Duke of Marlborough to Mr.
Brydges—Mr. Brydges appoints his deputy—The Rev.
Henry Brydges brings the "Darley" Arabian to England
—The Turkey Company.

THE family of Brydges, Bridges, Brigge, Bruges,
Burgh or Brugge, claims descent from Arnulp,
fifth and youngest son of Roger de Montgomery,
first Earl of Arundel and Shrewsbury, who led
the centre of Duke William's army at the battle
of Hastings. Arnulp—following the custom of
Cadets in those times—styled himself de Brugge,
after his father's castle in Shropshire. Such, in

B

brief, is the alleged Norman descent of the house, whose real founder was one Sir Simon de Brugge,—who flourished in the reigns of Henry III. and Edward I.,—and became lord of Bruge-Solers in Herefordshire, by his marriage with the heiress of the family of Solers. His grandson, Sir Thomas de Brugge, married Alice, daughter and co-heir of Sir Thomas Berkeley and Elizabeth his wife, daughter of Thomas, Lord Chandos. By this marriage some portion of the Chandos posses-sions was brought into the Brydges family. An ancestor in the fourth generation was the first of this family to be ennobled, being created, by Queen Mary in 1554, Baron Chandos of Sudeley, which manor and castle were granted him at the same time. This title in its eighth descent was inherited by James Brydges, cousin of the seventh lord, and father of James Brydges, afterwards the first Duke of Chandos.

James Brydges was born on the 6th day of January, 1673, and was baptized on the 12th of the same month at Dewsall, Herefordshire. After passing through the periods of childhood and ado-lescence without developing marked characteristics he was sent for the completion of his education as a Fellow Commoner to New College Hall, Oxford. Here he finished his studies, and displayed those powers of reflection and observation that ultimately made him famous. Before embarking on a public career he married Mary, daughter and afterwards heiress of Sir Thomas Lake of Canons near Edgware, Middlesex. In 1698 he entered the House of Commons as one of the members for Hereford. His family were no strangers to that Assembly; some of its members having sat for Cricklade, and the County of Gloucester, in previous reigns. In Edward II.'s time a Sir John de Brugge is recorded as one of the Knights of the Shire for the county of Hereford in the parliament held at York.

After a probation of three years, the heir to the Barony of Chandos—having obtained a footing in the political arena—acquired by assiduousness, coupled with a desire for office, some marks of favour at the hands of the House. On the 14th of June, 1701, he was deputed to carry up to the Lords the six articles of impeachment against Charles, Lord Halifax. The articles are so extraordinary that a brief *résumé* of them will not be out of place.

Article I. That he presumed to advise, pass or direct a grant to Thomas Railton, Esq., of forfeited estates and debts in Ireland, to the value of 13,000*l.*

Answer. His Lordship admitted he accepted the grant, as it was lawful for him to do, though it had been taken from him by Act of Parliament, thereby not making more than 400*l.* of it.

Article II. That he had not paid into the Exchequer of Ireland, as the Act of Forfeiture required, 1000*l.* that he had actually received out of the forementioned grants.

Answer. That monies received, being out of the mean profits (remitted by the Act), were not in the first mentioned clause of the same.

Article III. That he did obtain and accept several beneficial grants for himself, which was a monstrous abuse of his Majesty's goodness.

Answer. He admitted the acceptance of such grants, as marks of his Majesty's Royal favour.

Article IV. That he procured a grant to Henry Segar in trust for himself of 14,000*l.* worth of scrubbed beech, birch, etc., under colour of which, sapling oaks, and many trees of well-grown timber, had been cut and sold for his benefit.

Answer. He admitted a grant of 2000*l.* per annum for seven years, to be raised by the fall of scrubbed beech, etc., and if any abuse had been done in cutting the wood, he was not answerable for the same, such being done by the direction of his Majesty's Surveyor-General and other officers.

Article V. Appertains to the auditor's office.

Answer. He admitted having been one of the auditors of the Exchequer.

Article VI. Relates to the Partition Treaty.

Answer. He denied having advised his Majesty to make the treaty, nor was he even consulted on any of its clauses, though the subject was discussed at Tunbridge Wells, when he made several objections to the same.

An historian [1] of those times expresses surprise that such articles should be passed by an English House of Commons, and be carried up to the Peers. Their Lordships dismissed these impeachments against Lord Halifax on the 24th of June following (and a few days after the acquittal of John, Lord Somers, from the charges alleged in the articles exhibited against him).

Mr. Brydges, as a Whig, again played the part of champion against "Help yourself grants;" moving a resolution to the following effect:—

"That any minister who had been concerned in passing a grant for his own benefit, while the nation was under the heavy taxes of the late war, had vitiated his trust, etc., etc." This motion was most artfully contrived! Brought forward as an abstract truth (without naming Somers, or any one in particular), the House, by admitting it

[1] Oldmixon.

as a substantive resolution, would be compelled
to conclude that Lord Somers had violated his
trust by accepting King William's grant of Crown
property at Reigate. This conclusion the motion
was intended to convey. Sir Richard Gwyn fear-
lessly unmasked the attack, saying,[1] "Why this
reserve? everybody knows your meaning, and sees
you have not the courage to name the great man
whom you are seeking to destroy."

Mr. Brydges answered this declamation by
crying out, "That's false!" Thereon a violent
altercation ensued, and ultimately the House (in
this instance) refused to adopt so un-English
a procedure as the censure of a great minister,
vetoeing the resolution by a majority of 50 out
of 419 members present.

These two incidents occurred before Mr.
Brydges held any Government office.

One of the most important commissions Mr.
Brydges was appointed on, was that to inquire
into the accounts relating to the Earl of Ranelagh. The result of this examination by Brydges
and his fellow-commissioners, Messrs. H. St.
John, Bromley, Coke, Scobell, Copley and Byerley,
is best shown by the resolution passed by
the Commons on December 5th, 1703, to the

[1] Macaulay's History of England.

effect, " That it appears to this House that the
Earl of Ranelagh hath misappropriated several
sums of the public money." On the 1st of the
following February the Earl was expelled the
House.

That Mr. Brydges at this period was particularly careful of the National Exchequer, the following proves.[1]   One Thomas Wolfstenholme
petitioned the Lord High Treasurer *circa*
December 14th, 1703, as to certain sureties
accepted by him when receiver of duties from
the English plantations (he having lately
become insolvent), praying to be heard by
counsel, and proceedings stayed. Minute endorsed on petition, " My Lord will speak with
ye Commissioners next time they come." This
was read again on the 20th, when Mr. Attorney-
General said, " If he used the best endeavours,
and the sureties afterwards became insufficient,
the verdict would be for the petitioner."

But Mr. Brydges said that the sureties were
insufficient at the time, and the commissioners say
he took " insufficient securities."

To one presumably so anxious for the National
welfare as Mr. Brydges, it was apparent that
such openly expressed opinions against all forms

---

[1] Redington's Calendar of Treasury Papers.

of fraud must soon be rewarded with a lucrative
post. Therefore, so soon as the various govern-
mental changes under the new Sovereign, Anne,
were effected, Mr. Brydges was appointed, early
in 1705, an Auditor of the Imprest, and shortly
after was made Paymaster-General to the Forces
abroad. This latter appointment is frequently
mentioned as being bestowed in 1707. But a
congratulatory letter [1] from the Duke of Marlborough—who should know if anyone did who
was paymaster of his troops—proves the earlier
date to be correct.

The petition of Mr. Henry Cartwright,[2] dated
July 31st, 1705, testifies that Mr. Brydges was
then in full authority as paymaster. The petitioner prays the Lord High Treasurer to allow
him to accept the office of Deputy Paymaster-
General, offered him by Mr. Brydges. This he
could not do without his Lordship's permission,
being secretary to the controller of the accounts
for the army. If he might accept Mr. Brydges'
appointment, he could nominate a person to succeed him in the secretaryship, who would resign,
should he require the office again. This petition
is minuted (same date), " My Lord has nothing
to object against Mr. Brydges employing Mr.

[1] Vide App. A.   [2] Redington's Calendar of Treasury Papers.

Cartwright, but he cannot properly execute both employments ; therefore some other person must be appointed secretary to the comptrollers."

During this year, 1705, Mr. Brydges' brother, the Rev. Henry Brydges, being at Aleppo, was asked to take charge, on his voyage to England in the Turkey Company's ship *Ipswich* (commanded by Captain Watkins), of an Arabian horse, sent by Thomas Darley of that place, as a present to his brother, John Renter Darley of Aldby Park near York. This animal became known later as the celebrated Darley Arabian, whose blood still runs in some of our equine favourites.

Lord Chandos, father of the gentlemen above mentioned, was, in 1680, sent as [1] Ambassador to the Porte by the Levant—commonly known as the Turkey—Company : a large and wealthy Corporation, whose affairs he was interested in, having married a daughter of Sir Henry Barnard, an affluent Turkey merchant. This accounts no doubt for the Rev. Henry Brydges' presence on one of that Company's vessels, as well as for Mr. Thomas Darley's trust and obligation to him, as a son of one of its principal officers.

[1] This power the Company possessed by their Charter.

CHAPTER II.

MR. BRYDGES having obtained a lucrative appointment, that occupied much time and attention, his voice was now but little heard in the Commons.

Nor does much matter of interest occur during the first few years in which he held the office of Paymaster-General, with the exception of the following incidents which are briefly noticed. During 1706 Mr. Brydges went to Flanders, in connection with some mode or means of making remittances to the Forces. While there he appears to have misconstrued an order of the Lord High Treasurer's, respecting the profits on Exchange. This he acknowledges[1] in a letter dated Brussels, August 2nd, 1706, addressed to his lordship, in which he apologizes for mistaking his commands in reference to the profit on exchange, "And that he should look upon it as the greatest unhappiness that could befall him if any wrong interpretation he should make of his Lordship's orders, should create the least dissatisfaction imaginable to his Lordship, or his administration. He thought it best to make haste back to the army to prevent any wrong impressions."

Amongst other documents relating to Mr. Brydges (in the abstract of the Treasury[2] papers), is a letter dated October 7th, 1707, written by Mr. Brydges—but unaddressed — probably to some one in the Treasury. In it he apologizes for not making his acknowledgments sooner

[1] Redington's Calendar of Treasury Papers.   [2] Ibid.

—alleging the dispatch of business—and as a small instance of his gratitude, asks the acceptance of the "Bill" enclosed. This must not be read in the commercial sense of the present day, the bill being a bank bill or note, probably intended as a silver key.

On the 29th of the same month, October, 1707, complaint was made by Mr. Lowndes, that Mr. Brydges had neglected to send him fortnightly certificates of Receipts and Payments made to the forces. This, he points out, the Lord Treasurer had personally directed should be done, and requests that they be sent forthwith, as well as an account of the monies for the Forces in Spain. His demand, it is safe to assume, was complied with, as no further request for these documents appears.

Mr. Brydges received another mark of favour about this time, being called to the Council of Prince George of Denmark, in the affairs of the Admiralty. The appointment is alluded to in one of the Harleian MSS. entitled "Characters of Great Men in the early part of Queen Anne's Reign," thus :—

"James Brydges, Lord Chandos, was warm against King William's reign, nor does he make any great figure in this; but his son, Mr. Brydges, does, being of the House of Commons, one of the chancellors to the prince, and a very worthy gentleman."

Dean Swift, in his characters of the court of Queen Anne, enlarged upon this, calling Chandos "a very worthy gentleman, but a great complier with every court."

A remittance of 75,490l. was sent, on March 2nd, 1707-8, by Mr. Brydges to Mr. Morice, on account of the army in Spain,[1] with directions to send every farthing up to the person addressed, at the first opportunity. This would pay all the troops up to the end of June. All payments for the future must be for effectives only. . . . He further desired an account of all receipts and payments to be sent him, as this had been asked for several times by the Lord High Treasurer as well as by the parliament, who were not a little uneasy that winter, because no accounts had been returned. By this it appears that the pay of the Forces in Spain was in arrears, and that no vouchers had been submitted to the Treasurer, or the Commons. So matters progressed.

In the second parliament of Anne, 1708, Mr. Brydges met with some opposition in his second candidature for the City of Hereford. He was,

[1] Redington's Calendar of Treasury Papers.

however, ultimately returned, but not at the head
of the poll as in 1707, his former fellow-member,
Thomas Foley, being first favourite. Nevertheless, had Mr. Brydges been unsuccessful, the
representation of another constituency was kept
open for him by friends, who deemed Mr.
Brydges too useful a man to be out of parliament.   This opinion was likewise held by his,
then, friend, the Duke of Marlborough,[1] whose
communication to him at that period tends to
show that the Duke and Mr. Brydges perfectly
understood each other.   It is difficult to imagine
that Mr. Brydges could have held his appointment so long as he did, when Marlborough was
all powerful, had he not perfectly satisfied the
"Great Duke."

That the cares of office, coupled with parliamentary duties, did not exhaust all Mr. Brydges'
energies, is proved by his becoming a Fellow
of the Royal Society at this period.   The Royal
Society then consisted of a governing body of 20
Councillors together with 174 Fellows, of whom
50 were foreign members.   Mr. Brydges, however, is not recorded as taking such a part in
its affairs as would tend to interfere with his other
duties.

[1] Vide Appendix B.

The allusion made to the *entente cordiale* that existed between the Duke of Marlborough and Mr. Brydges is strengthened by a further communication [1] from his Grace. Its tenour shows that Mr. Brydges did not neglect to give the Duke his opinion on anything that transpired affecting him.

That Mr. Brydges, in a measure, changed the convictions he had held when he entered the House of Commons, is confirmed by his voting for the repeal of a clause in an Act passed the 13th and 14th of William III. and Mary II. intituled " An Act for the further limitations of the Crown," " or better securing the rights and liberties of the subject." The clause repealed by the second parliament of Anne was in these words, " That—after the limitations therein mentioned shall take effect—no person who has any office or place of profit under the king, or receives any pension from the crown, shall be capable of serving as a member of the House of Commons." This *in toto* was scarcely the essence of Mr. Brydges' contention in the impeachment of Lords Halifax and Somers : though the analogy is, that a person who professed such virtuous sentiments relative to the one case should do so in the other.

[1] Vide Appendix C.

On the 17th of October, 1709, Mr. Auditor
Harley reported to Earl Godolphin, Lord High
Treasurer, that he had examined the abstract of
payments made by Mr. Brydges to the forces
employed in the Low Countries during 1706, for
which payments warrants were wanting. He
likewise had examined the vouchers produced by
the accountant for proof of such payments. Also
that the abstract was the same as those of
previous accounts, relating to the aforesaid forces
for which Privy Seals had been granted; which
authority, he thinks, will be requisite for allowing
these.[1]   Here follow the various sums, amounting
to over half a million, with the purposes for
which they were disbursed; these are not now of
sufficient public interest to detail.   Accordingly,
in the July of the following year, the Solicitor-
General approved the draft for a Privy Seal to
pass the accounts.   But during the inquiry
into the state of the public accounts a year or so
later, Mr. Auditor Harley's report appears to
have been again gone into, as the following
endorsement shows :—"The above is a true copy
in the Honourable Mr. Auditor Harley's office of
the several payments, therein stated and proposed
to be allowed, and do appear to have been duly

[1] Newcastle MSS.

paid and applied by the accomptant, to the
services of the war, as by his accompts appear.

"Examined by

"JAS. MOODY, *Deputy Auditor.*"

"28th August, 1712."

This is the first mention of a Privy Seal, as
relating to Mr. Brydges' accounts, though not by
any means the last.

During the year 1710 more correspondence [1]
took place between his Grace of Marlborough
and Mr. Brydges, which further showed the
good feeling that existed between them.

Mr. Brydges, in reply to one of the Duke's
letters, announced his intention of applying for
an office held by Mr. Howe. But though the
Duchess seems to have considered Mr. Brydges
the man best suited for the position and recommended by her husband's friendship, she frustrated his application.[2]

Lord Treasurer Godolphin was dismissed
from office soon after, an event which caused
Mr. Brydges some anxiety. He quickly acquainted his Grace of Marlborough with the
fullest details of Godolphin's dismissal.

[1] Vide Appendix D.
[2] John Howe, Paymaster of the Forces at *Home.*

c

His Grace replied, expressing great concern at the news, on both public and private grounds; and approving Mr. Brydges' resolve not to resign his appointment on account of Lord Godolphin's dismissal. This correspondence further confirms the good relations that existed between the Commander-in-Chief and the Pay-master-General of the Forces abroad.

CHAPTER III.

Committee appointed by the Commons to inquire into the state of the public accounts—Report and discussion thereon —Allusion to, and statement showing the condition of Mr. Brydges' accounts—Mr. Brydges' residence in Albemarle Street damaged by fire—Continuation of correspondence with the Duke of Marlborough—His Grace continues to express regard for Mr. Brydges—Letter from Mr. St. John, Secretary for War, to Mr. Brydges— Reference to the Nicholas MSS., etc.—Letter from the Duke of Marlborough desiring to be supplied with any information that might interest him—Mr. Harley brings forward his South Sea scheme—Further report on Mr. Brydges' accounts—Letter from the Duke of Marlborough requesting Mr. Brydges' assistance in auditing payments made by Exchequer on account of Blenheim.

A COMMITTEE was shortly afterwards deputed by the House of Commons to inquire how far the several accountants had passed their respective accounts. Mr. Auditor Harley, on the 4th of April, 1711, handed the investigation to the House in the form of a report, which the committee directed him to make, whereupon it was ordered, " That it should be considered the following Tuesday; " when it was deferred first to the 17th, and afterwards to the 20th of the

same month.   The House then passed the
following resolution: "That of the monies
voted by parliament, and issued for the
public service to Christmas, 1710, they were
35,302,107*l*. 18*s*. 9*d*., for a great part whereof
no accounts had been laid before the auditors,
and the rest not prosecuted by the accountants
and finished."   The further consideration of the
report was put off till the 28th, when it was
further resolved, "That the not compelling the
several accountants to duly pass their respective
accounts, had been a notorious breach of trust in
those that of late years had had the management
of the Treasury, and an high injustice to the
nation."   A motion was thereupon framed and
put, "That the further consideration of the
report be adjourned."   This was negatived,
whereupon it was further resolved, "That the
several accountants ought no longer to be
entrusted with the public money."

Having given as succinctly as possible the
opinion of the Commons upon the state of the
public accounts, the question arises how far this
relates to Mr. Brydges.   The thirty-five millions
odd mentioned, consisted of some accounts as
far back as the time of Charles II.;[1] which

[1] Tindal.

were thrown in to make up the amount. The
largest item in the list, however, was the accounts
of Mr. Brydges, amounting to some millions,
of which scarcely one million had been passed,
though accounts of some eleven millions had
been presented but not passed in due form,
owing to the great care and exactness exercised
by the Duke of Newcastle,[1] whose duty it was to
pass accounts. This he was slow to do, allowing
nothing without hearing counsel on every item.
The real figures appertaining to Mr. Brydges'
office were as follows :—

"The Hon. James Brydges.

	£	s.	d.
His Charge is	£15,374,689	1	11¼

Discharge.

			£	s.	d.
By accounts passed	...	...	...	956,789	6	5¼
„ „ before auditors	...	...	8,097,492	8	7½
„ „ delivered since Christmas 1710	3,227,778	2	6
			12,282,059	17	6¾
To be accounted for	...	...	...	3,092,629	4	4½
			£15,374,689	1	11¼

[1] The Duke of Newcastle held at this time, amongst other
offices, that of Lord Privy Seal, hence the reason of such
of these accounts—as by the then rules of the Exchequer could
not be received without an authority under the Privy Seal at
least—being conducted at his office.—From Speaker Onslow's
notes on Burnet's History.

The foregoing implies nothing against Mr. Brydges at this time, though according to Dean Swift, during the debate on the matter, Mr. Secretary St. John was very zealous for his friend Mr. Brydges, upon whom part of the blame was falling, saying, "he did not know that either Mr. Brydges or the late ministry were at all to blame in the matter." The Dean affirms these words were very desperately spoken. So concluded the first report on the public accounts : this report was ordered to be printed; which, however, was not done, as it was found the report would indicate too pointedly those who had served both 'well and ill.'

In the early part of this year—1711—Mr. Brydges resided in Albemarle Street, next to Mr. Wyndham's, whose house was destroyed by fire, occasioning some damage to Mr. Brydges' residence.

The Duke of Marlborough and Mr. Brydges still continued their correspondence,[1] and in a communication from his Grace is found the first expression of discontent at Mr. Brydges' remittances on behalf of the forces under the Duke's command.

The zeal alluded to as being shown by Mr.

[1] Vide Appendix F.

Secretary St. John for his friend Mr. Brydges, during the debate on the state of the public accounts, doubtless led that gentleman to think that "one good turn deserved another," as he asked Mr. Brydges' kind offices in a matter relating to a Mr. Blake, with which he was much perplexed.[1] Mr. Brydges may safely be said to have performed this favour, as no other reference to it appears to have been made by Mr. St. John.

Allusions having been made to documents entitled the Nicholas papers, now in the Egerton collection of MSS., the reader is informed who that gentleman was and how far such papers are trustworthy. Edward Nicholas sat in the House of Commons for Shaftesbury, in the second parliament of Anne, afterwards holding an appointment in the Treasury. During the absence of Dr. Robinson, Bishop of Bristol, Lord Privy Seal, at the Peace of Utrecht in 1711 the office of Lord Privy Seal was for the time held under commission by Sir Joseph Beaumont, Robert Byerly and Edward Nicholas, esquires. The last-mentioned gentleman was later appointed Treasurer and Paymaster of her Majesty's pensioners. Mr. Nicholas's father had also held

[1] Vide Appendix G.

various appointments under Government at an earlier date. Mr. Nicholas thus had many opportunities for acquiring precise information, particularly with respect to matters concerning the army.

That Mr. Brydges kept the Duke of Marlborough well informed on subjects affecting their relative positions, is evidenced by a letter [1] from his Grace, wherein he desires a continuance of information.

On the 2nd of May, 1711, Mr. Harley brought forward in the House of Commons, whilst in committee upon Ways and Means, his famous motion for the formation of the South Sea scheme. As this bubble had later some bearing on the fortunes of Mr. Brydges, the sum of Mr. Harley's proposal is here briefly stated. He proposed to relieve the public of all National Debts by allowing the proprietors of such securities interest at the rate of six per cent. per annum (redeemable by vote of parliament), giving them, in addition, a charter of incorporation, conferring a monopoly of the trade to the South Seas. The supposition was that the islands when settled would yearly bring to Great Britain vast riches from Mexico and Peru. It is now

[1] Vide Appendix H.

a matter of history how this wild scheme was passed and adopted from the 24th of December of that year.[1]

With respect to the state of Mr. Brydges' accounts at this period, the following report was made by the auditors to the Lord Treasurer, wherein it is stated that the Privy Seal—previously mentioned—for allowing some of the payments made without warrant, had not yet reached their hands, although the draft for its issue had been approved by the Solicitor-General.[2]

"To the Right Honourable Robert, Earl of Oxford and Mortimer, Lord High Treasurer of Great Britain."

"May it please your Lordship.

"By your Lordship's order of reference upon the annexed memorandum of the Honourable James Brydges, Esquire, we are directed to let your Lordship know in what forwardness his accounts are, and to request our opinion in what may be fit for you to do therein, for obedience thereunto we humbly acquaint your Lordship :—

"That Mr. Brydges has delivered in his accounts from Midsummer, 1705, to Christmas, 1709. The first of them goes to Christmas, 1705, in Ireland.

[1] See also page 113.
[2] Nicholas papers, Egerton MSS.

The next account ending Christmas, 1706, stops
only for want of a Privy Seal, a draft of which lay
before the late Lord Privy Seal, with Sir Edward
Northey's opinion thereon, for the passing of it,
but it is not yet come to us under seal.   That
pursuant to the late Lord Treasurer's directions
of the 30th of June, 1710, upon reading our
report on an abstract of payments made by the
said Mr. Brydges for the service of the war in
Holland, between the 24th of December, 1706,
and the 23rd of December, 1707, for which warrants were wanting, we did then prepare and
lay before his Lordship such a draft of a warrant
as we thought proper, in order to the passing the
Privy Seal, for allowing the sums mentioned in
the said report.   A copy of which report and
warrant we herewith lay before your Lordship.

"We are also preparing a report which will
soon be laid before your Lordship, of such of the
payments for the year 1708 as need the authority
of a Privy Seal, and his accounts for the year
1709 are under examination.   All of which is
humbly submitted.

> "E. HARLEY.
> "H. MAYNWARING.

"October 1st, 1711."

This document bears endorsement, at back, as follows: "Statements of the two auditors upon the state of Mr. Brydges' accounts, dated October 1st, 1711."

The foregoing shows that the audit of Mr. Brydges' accounts was still wearily dragging along. In fact, tardiness seems to have ruled triumphant; whether for caution or as a cloak to deficiencies, subsequent events may tend to show.

On the same date as the above-mentioned report was made, the Duke of Marlborough despatched a letter[1] to Mr. Brydges, asking his assistance in auditing the payments made by the Exchequer for the erection of Blenheim. As the Duke soon after returned to England, this communication is the last one recorded as having passed between them during his Grace's absence as Commander-in-Chief of the Forces abroad.

The request contained in this letter shows that the Duke fully reciprocated the sentiments expressed by Mr. Brydges; as his Grace of Marlborough would scarcely have asked such a favour at the hands of one who did not share his fullest confidence. Moreover, the matter involved was not in any way connected with Mr. Brydges' Office. Probably his Grace thought of this when

[1] Vide Appendix I.

requesting the obligation, and thus endeavoured
to procure an independent audit.   It must, however, be admitted that the sentiments expressed in
the preamble of this communication are most
praiseworthy, and show that the Duke wished to
be exact.

CHAPTER IV.

ON the 21st December, 1711, the Commissioners
for examining the public accounts made a further
report to the House of Commons on some prac-
tices they had discovered relating to the affairs
of the army.   Mr. Lockhart read the report from
his seat, and afterwards handed it to the Clerk at
the table.

The discovery made by the Commissioners was
that the Duke of Marlborough had received from
Sir Solomon de Medina, Contractor for bread to
the Forces in the Low Countries, during the
years 1707-11, a sum of money for his own use,

on each contract, amounting in the aggregate to some 332,425 guilders, 14 stivers. Sir Solomon deposed that it appeared from the accounts of Antonio Alvarez Machado, the contractor, who supplied the forces for the years 1702-6, that he had paid similar sums to his Grace, during the period he was contracting; these, with the amount previously stated, made a total of 664,851 guilders 8 stivers : a sum, at the then current rate of exchange, equivalent to 63,410*l.* 3*s.* 7*d.* In addition to this payment to the Duke, he had to give Mr. Cardonnell, his Grace's secretary, a *douceur* of 500 ducats in gold, upon each contract being sealed, and when he came to receive payment for his supplies he had to further submit to a deduction by Mr. Sweet, deputy-paymaster at Amsterdam, of a commission of 1 per cent.

The Duke of Marlborough, having heard of Sir Solomon's denouncement, wrote to the commissioners from the Hague, under date of November 10th, 1711, to the effect that the sums so received were no more than what had been always allowed, as a perquisite to the General commanding the army in the Low Countries; and further asserted that whatever sums had been so received were expended in the public service, for

secret intelligence, and referred to a deduction of
2½ per cent., (for which he held her Majesty's
warrant), from the pay of the foreign troops
under English colours, for defraying extraordinary expenses relating to them.   This deduction, he averred, had been made a free gift to him
by the Allies, concluding, that he deemed the
service of the army in Flanders had been carried
on with all possible economy.

The Commissioners adverted upon the Duke's
letter at some length, and denied the latter part
of the Duke's contention : that the deductions had
been carried out in the strict sense of the royal
warrant, which directed that the deduction should
be made and held by the Paymaster or his deputy,
and issued thence by the Duke's order only.
This method does not appear by the Paymaster's
accounts to have been pursued.   On the contrary, such payments seem to have been made in
full to the foreign troops ; also, Mr. Brydges had
stated on oath, that he had never seen any warrant
for the purpose specified, or knew anything, as
Paymaster, of such deduction.   On the other
hand, if Mr. Sweet, the Deputy Paymaster at
Amsterdam, had thought fit to transact the disposition of this 2½ per cent.,[1] with the Duke, the

[1] Amounting to a sum of 177,000*l.*

Commissioners held that he ought to have sent
regular accounts of such payment to Mr.
Brydges, whose only agent he was, and should
certainly not have negotiated such large sums of
public money clandestinely.

So far as can be ascertained, Mr. Brydges' explanation appears to have destroyed the good
feeling hitherto existing between his Grace and
himself, for no continuance of these friendly
epistles are recorded in the volumes[1] containing
copies of the Duke's correspondence ; nor is it
to be gathered from other sources.

The result of this report was the declaration
by the Queen in Council on the 30th of the same
month, " That being informed that information
against the Duke of Marlborough had been laid
before the Commons by the Commissioners of
public accounts, she thought fit to dismiss him
from all his employments, so that the matter might
take an impartial examination," though her
Majesty personally wrote to the Duke the day
following, " That her intention was to reserve all
the employments she had entrusted him with,
etc., etc." But this was never fulfilled, as his
Grace retired abroad, residing first at Frankfort,
and afterwards at Antwerp. Having at last

[1] Murray's Marlborough's Letters and Despatches, 1845.

resolved to return to his native land, he arrived on the day of her Majesty's decease.

King George I., soon after his accession, re-appointed his Grace Commander-in-Chief; but the appointment did not carry the power he had previously enjoyed.

With the advent of the year 1712, Mr. Brydges formed those resolutions which ultimately resulted in the raising of one of the most sumptuous and costly mansions ever erected in this country. It has been stated previously that Mr. Brydges married Mary, daughter, and ultimately heiress of Sir Thomas Lake, grandson of the Secretary of State to that modern Solomon, King James I. Sir Thomas had purchased the estate of Canons, near Edgware, Middlesex, from Sir Hugh Losse. The estate ultimately came into the possession of Mr. Brydges, through his wife, as aforesaid. It was here that he finally determined to erect an edifice, the fame of which the Muse of that note of interrogation "Pope" has handed down to posterity. Canons, however, was not the first site selected by Mr. Brydges. Owing to a disagreement with the owner of Sion House, some land a little to the north of Brentford was relinquished; though the pillars for the gates were still standing 100 years later.

D

There is much doubt as to the exact date when the foundations of Canons were commenced. Some authorities date *circa* 1712; others 1715. After mature deliberation, my opinion is that the latter is most likely correct, for many reasons. One of the most important of these is that in 1712 Mr. Brydges still held his appointment as Paymaster-General; and however lucrative that office may have been made by him, it would have been little short of madness to have commenced the erection of a noble and costly palace while he held a position that had already been the subject of question in the House of Commons. Besides, such an undertaking immediately following the dismissal of the Duke of Marlborough must have drawn attention to the emoluments of Mr. Brydges' post. Another good reason in favour of the later date is that by this period he had succeeded his father as Lord Chandos. He could, therefore, with better grace, commence a lordly residence, as a peer of the realm, even if previously enriched by fruits of office. Besides, the Committee for inspecting the state of the public accounts had then ceased its labours.

That there were other difficulties in connection with Mr. Sweet's office as Deputy Paymaster, is

made evident by a communication [1] from his senior
(Mr. Brydges), to the Lord Treasurer, enclosing
Mr. Sweet's reasons for not protesting Sir John
Lambert's bills of exchange for 312,000 florins,
current money of Holland, and requesting his
Lordship's direction thereon.

On the 10th of June, 1712, a report [2] was made
by Messrs. Levinge and Bernard, respectively
Attorney and Solicitor Generals for Ireland, to
the Lords Justices, relating to a pension of 500*l.*
per annum, granted to the Earl of Granard.
This, it was contended, had been sold to Anthony
Hammond, Esq.—Mr. Brydges' deputy at the pay
office—for 1600*l.*, and afterwards resold by him
to Mr. Brydges.   The earl's contention was, that
he had only mortgaged it to Mr. Hammond, and
not sold or assigned it absolutely.   On certain
conditions, he prayed that the stop placed on the
payment of the pension might be removed, and
this petition was granted.   It is not assumed that
the transaction was a matter of arrangement
between Mr. Brydges and his deputy, though it
does appear strange, that almost so soon as Mr.
Hammond had acquired what appears to be a
bargain, it should be transferred to Mr. Brydges,

[1] Redingtons' Calendar of Treasury Papers.   [2] Ibid.

his senior. Possibly other instances, that will be recorded of the latter's dealing with offices and grants, may help to enlighten the reader's mind on this subject.

Owing to the investigations made by the committee appointed to inquire into the Duke of Marlborough's affairs, and other matters connected with the Army, and the consequent disclosures, the following command was sent Mr. Brydges by H. St. John, then Secretary for War :—

[1] " To the Honourable JAMES BRYDGES,

"Paymaster-General of the Forces,

"Whitehall.

"June 21st, 1712.

"SIR,—Her Majesty has thought fit to order that payment should be stopped of all pay or subsidies to the foreign troops on her Service, till further notice, which you will be pleased to signify without loss of time to Mr. Sweet, and at the same time, to direct him to issue no pay to any foreigners serving in the Low Countries, till he shall receive directions so to do from his Grace the Duke of Ormonde, and from the Earl of

[1] Parkes' Life of Henry St. John, Viscount Bolingbroke.

Strafford, who is going away to-morrow to the Army in Flanders. The orders must be positive, and her Majesty expects they should be punctually complied with. My Lord Treasurer desires me to acquaint you, that the messenger who goes to Holland, stays at my office for your letter, which he is to carry with him. You will please therefore, as soon as this comes to your hand, to write accordingly to Mr. Sweet, deputy paymaster to the Army in Flanders, and to send your letter to my office, that the messenger may be despatched with it.

"I am, Sir,

"Your most humble servant,

"H. St. John."

It would be difficult to find a letter which better exemplifies the maxim *Suaviter in modo, fortiter in re,* or which more plainly manifests the iron hand under the silk glove. Not only is the command courteously though imperatively worded for immediate compliance, but keeping the messenger at Mr. St. John's office for Mr. Brydges' letter, was a master stroke of policy, to command obedience and prevent delay.

CHAPTER V.

THE Commissioners for examining the state of the public accounts were still holding their inquiries, though unable to reach the accounts more directly concerning Mr. Brydges in the current year.

Although Mr. Brydges had decided ultimately to make the family domain of the Lake the place whereon to rear his costly mansion, it was fated that the descendant of that family — Mrs. Brydges—should not live to see her husband's mansion erected on the estate of her ancestors. She died in the December of 1712.

It is frequently stated that Mr. Brydges vacated the office of Paymaster-General to the Forces abroad during the year just named. That this date was anticipatory, will be presently shown.

On April, 16th, 1713, the Commissioners again

reported to the House the result of their investigations. These were briefly :—That they were forced to omit many particulars for want of examining the deputy paymasters, Mr. Sweet and Mr. Morice, on oath, through whose hands most of the public money had passed. Mr. Sweet; the deputy, could not give a satisfactory explanation of some mismanagement at Amsterdam. Therefore a *precept* was sent for his attendance here (though in the meantime he was dismissed from his office), when he requested an indulgence of six months before returning to England. The reasons not being deemed adequate, request was again made for his immediate attendance with such books and papers as would enable him to give an exact account of all the monies received and paid during the war in the Low Countries. Thereupon he repeated his previous answer, and it was feared that no personal information could be obtained from him, without the interposition of Parliament.

Mr. Morice, the deputy in Portugal, having recently died, the Commissioners' intention of looking into his accounts was frustrated. But the Paymaster-General, Mr. Brydges, had sent a person to Lisbon to prepare them. Mr. Mead, the deputy in Spain, having only just arrived in this country, they had as yet been unable to go through his accounts.

One point in the great mismanagement of the army was that of paying regiments without establishments. The paymaster-general declared on oath before the Commissioners :—" That the regiments of Hogon, D'Assa, and Dalzel, were paid by authority of the general's warrant alone." The Commissioners also found : " That some regiments had been paid which were never on any establishments, while others had been paid before they were established.

" The Earl of Galway's Spanish regiment. . . we have received so very an uncertain account of, that there seems to have been unnecessary expense made on the public for providing it. Captain Henry Pullein deposes that he held a captain's commission dated April 6th,1709, given him by the Earl of Galway; that he arrived in Portugal the June following, when he heard the regiment had been taken prisoners, and found two or three officers there, but never saw any privates, nor did he hear that any musters were ever taken. The commissary, and the paymaster-general have deposed :—That they never saw any muster rolls, but that there was a list of prisoners returned to the paymaster, after the regiment was supposed to have been taken by the enemy, wherein the name of only one private is inserted, which has created the suspicion, that the regiment was an imaginary one and never actually raised.

" Some regiments have been placed on several establishments at the same time, Farrington's, for instance, on three, viz., Flanders, Spain, and Portugal; Mordaunt's and Macartney's, in the same manner; Hill's and Hotham's were put in both estimates (for Spain and Portugal), and twice provided for by parliament. The sum of 90,954*l*. 19*s*. 2*d*. was given in excess for these five regiments than was applied to their use. But Mr. Brydges alleges that part of the sum allotted to the regiments of Mordaunt, Farrington and Macartney, was issued for the pay of SOME Foreign Corps.

" Other regiments have been paid different from their respective establishments: Elliott's was placed on the Flanders establishment at 44*l*. 11*s*. 4*d*. *per diem*, but was paid by Mr. Brydges at the rate of 39*l*. 15*s*. 8*d*., those of Lalo, Farrington, and Macartney at 42*l*. 10*s*. 0*d*., paid by Mr. Brydges at 39*l*. 8*s*. 2*d*., that of Mordaunt's at 42*l*. 10*s*. 0*d*. was paid at the rate of 39*l*. 6*s*. 2*d*.; Blisset's at 36*l*. 10*s*. 2*d*. paid at the rate of 32*l*. 10*s*. 2*d*. From this it is plain that a considerable sum was voted by parliament, more than was applied to the service, or is yet otherwise accounted for.

"As the above mentioned regiments have received less than their establishment, so that of Carles has received 1819*l*. 13*s*. 6*d*. more, being placed on the establishment at 28*l*. 18*s*. 6*d*. *per diem*, and paid at the rate 42*l*. 10*s*. 0*d*.

"The above are so far as Mr. Brydges' office was directly concerned, though there were other. . . allegations affecting the forces at home, and the Navy." The Commissioners report that they had noticed the sale of public offices and called the attention of the House thereto, and cited two instances; the first directly refers to Mr. Brydges.

"Henry Meriton Esq., in 1705, treated with Mr. Brydges, then Auditor of the Imprests, for the purchase of his office, agreeing to give 4000*l*. for it, and thereon applied to the Lord Treasurer Godolphin for his approbation. His lordship proposed to make him Commissioner of Customs, or Cashier of the Excise, in consideration of the 4000*l*. he was to pay Mr. Brydges. But he absolutely refused the first proposal, and was with great difficulty brought to accept the latter office considering the terms too hard, as the office was given during pleasure only. However, being persuaded by Sir William Scawen, to rely on the Lord Godolphin's honour, he paid Mr. Brydges the 4000*l*., whereon Mr. Maynwaring was made Auditor of the Imprests. Mr. Hall, Cashier of the Excise, was removed from that office to be a Commissioner of the Customs; and Mr. Meriton entered into the Excise as cashier. By this it is evident that Lord Godolphin was not only privy to this bargain and sale, but negotiated it. However, the Commissioners examined Mr. Maynwaring on oath, who deposed that his Lordship transacted the whole matter without his knowledge. But he heard that a sum of money was given to Mr. Brydges on resigning his office. As a further confirmation of this, when Mr. Meriton was dismissed in 1710 from being Cashier of the Excise, he remonstrated with Lord Godolphin, saying that ' he could not sit down with the loss of 4000*l*;' and insisted on his lordship's promise of continuing the post to him. His lordship apprehending himself under an obligation to reimburse Mr. Meriton, as he was pleased to say for his own sake, means were found, on making Colonel Sidney Comptroller of the Excise, to raise 4000*l*. for Mr. Meriton by a cross sale of those offices."

This concluded the substance of the first report. But on the same day a second one was handed in, of which the following is a *resumé :—*

" The Commissioners humbly submit by what is offered in the preceding report, that they will be deemed to have taken some pains in examining the accounts of the army, and for having used all possible endeavours to detect any irregularities or mismanagements therein. Mr. Howe,[1] in return to our *precept,* brought in accounts of some regiments, but, in examination thereof, we found that they had reference to other accounts— while those regiments were in Mr. Brydges' pay— which are unadjusted.

" Mr. Brydges also exhibited to us, some time since, the state of several regiments, but alleged that there were so many difficulties in their accounts, that he could not settle the credits of any one of them. The colonels and agents have returned that, till the credits of their respective regiments are fixed by the PAYMASTER, they cannot pretend to offer any accounts. As these have been numerous, it is hoped they will facilitate our examinations when the paymasters are prepared to lay their accounts before us in such a manner as will form a proper foundation for

---

[1] John Howe, Paymaster of the Forces at home.

us to determine on. Mr. Brydges has been frequently pressed to attest the credits of the regiments under his care, as they form the most considerable part of the army; but, being unable to remove the difficulties first complained of, he has lately delivered on oath to us a paper entitled, 'Reasons why the accounts for the regiments under the care of the Honourable James Brydges, Esquire, Paymaster-General of her Majesty's Forces, acting in conjunction with the Allies, could not be closed and attested, pursuant to the *precepts* of the Honourable Commissioners appointed by parliament for taking, examining, and determining the debts due to the army, etc. Dated, March 4th, 1712-13.

"Now whether these reasons are admitted as a justification of the paymaster or otherwise, your Commissioners apprehend they are a sufficient proof, that it was not in their power to proceed further than they have done.

" (Signed)

"GEORGE LOCKHART, HENRY BERTIE, SOLWAY WINNINGTON, FRANCIS ANNESLEY, THOMAS LISTER, WILLIAM SHIPPEN, HENRY CARTER."

The House having heard Mr. Shippen read these Reports from his seat in the Commons, it

was resolved to take them into consideration on
the Saturday following. At the same time they
ordered a Bill to be brought in, " To revive and
continue the Act for taking, examining and
stating the public accounts, and to continue the
Act for appointing Commissioners to examine
debts due to the army."

However painstaking the Commissioners may
have been, the results of their labours amount
almost to *nil*. True, they were baffled and foiled
at almost every step, as if some master mind was
directing the mystification. An important con-
tribution towards the elucidation of these accounts,
would have been the discovery as to who was
really responsible for, or initiated the dismissal
of Mr. Sweet, the deputy at Amsterdam, without
first bringing his accounts to this country, as immediately he received his discharge (by letter),
he perfectly well knew what to expect on
returning here. In other words, he should have
been temporized with. His absence—as they this
side knew—would prevent any direct allegations
being made by the committee, against those in
the pay office at Whitehall. The death of Mr.
Morice, Mr. Brydges' deputy in Portugal, naturally prevented the Commissioners receiving that
gentleman's personal testimony, relative to the

accounts under his charge. The same reason will apply to the alleged sale of " offices," the late Lord Treasurer Godolphin dying whilst the Commission was sitting.

The above, coupled with the form of the second report, prevented any specific charge being made against Mr. Brydges. At the most, the allegations made were general ones, so much so, that they could not fix any one with any of the many irregularities stated to exist in the office of Mr. Brydges, though the Commissioners were morally certain that the country had been, and was being, defrauded to an enormous extent.

That Mr. Brydges was a clever and fortunate man, is proved by the turn events were made to take. He showed great circumspection, by not (at this time) making a parade of his wealth, by adopting that style of magnificence which he did later. His good fortune permitted him to escape directly or indirectly, the censure of the Commons (as in the case of Sir Robert Harley and others). In fact his position in the House does not appear to have been affected in the least by the Commissioners' reports, as he was returned at the head of the poll for Hereford, his old seat, in the new Parliament. Mr. Brydges possessed in a marked degree the faculty of making himself agreeable to all with whom he was brought into contact. In fact, he studied, and acted up to the motto, " *Noblesse Oblige*," and showed frequently magnanimous conduct in support of that maxim. Such a disposition naturally stood him in good stead at the present juncture, particularly with a grave though legally unproved charge hanging over him. But even this did not prevent him, at a later period, from being named as a probable commissioner to aid in carrying on a still higher trust.

Mr. Smollett in his continuation of Hume's History of England, asserts in reference to the accounts of the army appertaining to Mr. Brydges' office, " That all means had proved ineffectual to determine and punish those individuals who shamefully pillaged their country. The villainy was so complicated, the vice so general, and the delinquents so powerfully screened by artifice and interest, as to elude all inquiry." This has been shown in these pages, even more conclusively than the historian asserts. Smollett further states, that Mr. Brydges accounted for all the monies that passed through his hands except three millions; an assertion which no doubt has reference to the figures previously given.

For this sum Mr. Brydges had to produce accounts or vouchers. As several audits followed, it is safe to assume that this sum was wholly or in part accounted for. It is not denied that Mr. Brydges acquired a handsome fortune during his tenure of office as Paymaster-General, though what this amounted to no one ever knew. Three millions, however, is far too large a sum to estimate it at, great even as Mr. Brydges' expenditure was, after his official retirement from the Pay Office. In building and other acquisitions, however, he both made and lost large amounts by various schemes, though all of these would hardly reach the seven-figured sum stated. It must also be remembered that he was then in possession of the family estates; these alone would have enabled him to keep up a fair establishment.

CHAPTER VI.

NOTWITHSTANDING the report of the Commissioners, Mr. Brydges still retained his appointment. This is proved by his presenting to the House of Commons, May 2nd, 1713, an estimate of what was due for the clearings and set-off reckonings of her Majesty's troops, upon the establishments of Spain, Portugal, and the Low Countries, from the time they were last paid till March 25th, 1713. The title being read, it was ordered, " That the said estimate do lie upon the table of the House to be perused by the members."

It appears that one of the results of the Inquiry into the state of the public accounts, was the making many of the offices alluded to by the Commissioners, a little more circumspect in conducting their affairs ; this appears from the following letter :—

[1] " Whitehall, 18th July, 1713.

" GENTLEMEN,—I enclose to you a copy of my Lord Duke of Ormonde's letter to me, by which you will see his Grace is of opinion the troops ought to be paid according to the muster rolls. I desire you will please lay the same before my Lord Treasurer for his Lordship's directions, whether the same must be paid according to the muster or effective lists. The Act of Parliament being so express in directing the former, and being renewed the last sessions, I humbly submit whether the paying by any other authority will not be an infringement of that Act.

" I am, gentlemen,

" Your most humble servant,

" J. BRYDGES.

" Secretary to the Treasury."

[1] From MSS. relating to the Army, 1698—1715.

This letter testifies that Mr. Brydges was moving cautiously; he was about to resign office, and was naturally desirous of quitting his post with as good a grace as possible.

Notwithstanding the worry and anxiety of this year—1713—Mr. Brydges found leisure to woo and win a second wife. This lady was Cassandra, daughter of Sir F. Willoughby, and sister of the then newly created Lord Middleton; she was also a first cousin of Mr. Brydges, and related to Earl Tylney, the erector of the once splendid pile of Wanstead. Mr. Brydges espoused his second wife on the 4th of August, 1713. The ceremony took place in the chapel attached to the Royal Military Hospital, Chelsea, probably selected on account of Mr. Brydges' connection with the civil establishment of the army.

One of the many reasons why the post of Paymaster to the Forces was so lucrative in those times, consisted in the very large sums of money that frequently lay for some time in the Paymaster's hands, before the period arrived for its disbursement. This is alluded to as a fact in connection with that office, and not as reflecting on anyone who held the appointment. It was looked upon as one of the emoluments of

the post, that the money should be lucratively
used for the time, to the paymaster's advantage.

Amongst the several papers [1] consulted for this
work, is a document elaborately drawn up to
show what would be necessary for carrying on
the service to Christmas, and paying the bills of
exchange in Mr. Brydges' office, 1712-13. The
sum for meeting these expenses amounts to
869,134*l.* There is in Mr. Brydges' hands (or
intended to be issued to him) the following :—

1710.

General mortgage, subscribed to :	£
South Sea Company	409,600
Land Tax	73,895
Malt „	7,558
Candle Tax	7,500
	498,553

1711.

Land Tax	24,500
Malt „	80,975
Hops „	30,346
South Sea Stock	151,300
In money to be received from the Two Millions voted . .	132,162
	£917,836

showing an estimated surplus of 48,702*l.*, which
is subsequently swallowed up by other items to

[1] MSS. relating to the Army, 1698—1715.

be provided for, ultimately resulting in a debit of 63,433*l*. These accounts are curious, as showing the ways and means then employed for providing the army. Nor will it escape observation that a large proportion of the money in hand was invested in South Sea stock, though this period is previous to that of the inflated condition.

A Mr. Thomas Moore is recorded as succeeding Mr. Brydges in the office of Paymaster-General during the year 1713, although the latter's connection with that post does not appear to have entirely ceased. On April 7th, 1714,[1] Mr. Brydges presented to the House of Commons by her Majesty's commands (pursuant to their address for that purpose), an account of several charges for H.M. forces, which are not provided for in Mr. Brydges' office between the 22nd of December, 1712, and the 24th of August, 1713. These accounts consist of thirteen items, relating to pay of regiments, etc., and expenses of the Commander-in-Chief in Portugal, and amount to 71,473*l*. 12*s*. 11¼*d*. This appears to have been the last official statement presented by him to the House of Commons, though for some years inquiries and references were made to

[1] House of Commons Journal, vol. xvii.

him by officials in the Treasury and other depart-
ments.

Mr. Brydges, being now relieved from the
cares of office, began to put into execution those
plans that he had determined upon, so soon as
time and other circumstances allowed. He
also resolved to add to his landed possessions
in the neighbourhood of Canons as opportunity
arose, so as to make his power as great as
possible in the vicinity of his contemplated
princely residence. One of the first steps he took
was to purchase, during the year 1714, the
assignment of the unexpired term of the Ranger-
ship of Enfield Chace, Middlesex, then a lordly
domain, some twenty-one miles in circumference.
Enfield Chace had been granted in 1694 for a
term of fifty-six years to Sir Robert Howard,
who afterwards assigned it. This assignee, in his
turn, sold it to Mr. Brydges, in whose family it
remained for several generations.

As a means towards the spiritual welfare of
himself and neighbours, he presented the living
of Whitchurch—close to Canons—to the learned
John Theophilus Desaguliers, LL.D., F.R.S.,
son of the Rev. John Desaguliers, a French
refugee, educated at Christ Church, Oxford.
This gentleman was held in high favour by Sir

Isaac Newton, and was the first person who gave
public lectures in London upon Experimental
Philosophy. The lectures, together with other
works of a scientific nature, were afterwards
published by him.

Having presented the living of Whitchurch
to an esteemed friend and brother F.R.S., whom
he also made his chaplain, Mr. Brydges did what
a magnanimous patron would do under such circumstances ; he presented the new incumbent (and
parishioners) with a new church. He proposed
to make the church's decorations similar to the
intended private chapel at Canons, and worthy of
proximity to his purposed princely edifice. The
date of the commencement of the latter building is here confirmed, for it is a fact that the
church of St. Lawrence was pulled down—except
the tower—in 1715, although its re-erection
progressed slowly owing to the same artists
and workmen being simultaneously engaged at
Canons.

During the last days of her Majesty Queen Anne,
the Earl of Oxford, who was Lord Treasurer, was
removed from office. The event was so sudden
that much strife and confusion ensued, particularly as no substitute had been agreed upon.
Hasty consultation was therefore held ; when it

was proposed that the office of treasurer should be executed by a [1] commission of five. Sir William Wyndham, of the Exchequer, was to be one, but the choice of the others was somewhat puzzling to her Majesty, as well as her councillors. It is said that the persons mentioned were the Lords Bolingbroke, Paget, Lexington, Bathurst, and Masham, the Bishop of London, the Honourables Henry Boyle, and James Brydges, together with many others; but no definite selection was then made. It would seem that Mr. Brydges was still regarded with confidence amongst the powers that were, his name being mentioned as a possible commissioner for so important an office as the Treasury.

On the 16th of October, 1714, James, Lord Chandos, died at his seat of Aconbury, near Hereford, and was succeeded by his son James. The late lord had been one of the seven barons, or viscounts, selected for promotion to the degree of earl, upon the accession of his Majesty King George I. The names of these noblemen were Chandos, Ossulton, Guernsey, Halifax, Rockingham, Harvey and Pelham; but Lord Chandos died before the official announcement of his Majesty's favour was made, and his

---

[1] Afterwards put into effect.

son and successor received the honour intended
for the father.   On the 19th of October, 1714,
it was announced that the Right Honourable
James Brydges, Lord Chandos, was to be
created Viscount Wilton, of Wilton, Herefordshire, and Earl of Carnarvon ; the letters patent
to be entailed on his brother the Honourable
and Rev, Henry Brydges, in default of surviving
male issue.   The foregoing explanation clears up
much doubt that has arisen; as many have
wished to know why Mr. Brydges, a person supposed to have greatly enriched himself at the
public cost, was one of the first to receive
favour from the hands of the new sovereign.
The newly-created Earl lost no time in attaching
himself to the court, as well as to the interests
of his Majesty King George I.   In fact he
thoroughly foreshadowed—except in meanness—
Macklin's character of Sir Pertinax McSyco-
phant in *The Man of the World*, who always
" Boo'd boo'd where the sun shone."

Mention might here be made of the Earl's
political convictions, which were, as they had
been during his parliamentary career, those of
the Whig party.   Though nevertheless a fact,
this assertion may probably raise a doubt in the
reader's mind.   Nor is it such a difficult matter to

prove, as the Whigs from the accession of Anne to the beginning of the reign of George III. were such in name only, having, during the intervening reigns, acted and voted as Tories.

Mr. Brydges, now Earl of Carnarvon, though relegated to the House of Peers, was frequently referred to in matters relating to his late office. Thus on the 27th October,[1] 1714,[1] a petition was presented by Mr. Hill and another, respecting charges for provisions. This is minuted to be considered when another Privy Seal passes for my Lord Carnarvon. On the 27th of the following month Mr. Morice, executor to his father, the late deputy paymaster to the forces in Portugal, presented a petition in reference to certain charges for shipping money from Lisbon to Catalonia, minuted to be read when my Lord Carnarvon and Mr. Auditor Harley are at the Treasury. These were not the last queries that arose concerning the Earl's late appointment as Paymaster.

After succeeding to the family honours, Lord Carnarvon desired that his late seat for Hereford in the Commons should be filled by a person of his own political views, especially as that constituency had honoured him with their suffrages on behalf of

[1] Redington's Calendar of Treasury Papers.

the Whig party during eight Parliaments. With
this purpose he strenuously supported the candidature of Messrs. Westfaling and Philpotts for
that party. They and their supporters were surprised to find themselves opposed by Viscount
Scudamore, who, instead of seeking re-election for
the County, had, at the earnest solicitation of the
electors, determined to contest the City of Hereford, in conjunction with Thomas Foley, one of
its late members, in the Tory interest. In this
they were successful, the poll being for,[1]—

Thomas Foley	787
Viscount Scudamore	777
Westfaling	575
Philpotts	551

Such a result was not anticipated by the Earl,
who throughout the election felt confident that
one of his candidates would obtain the suffrages
of those electors whose political sentiments cor-
responded with his own, and who, for so long a
time, had shown their allegiance to him.

[1] This circumstance, added to others of a political character,
so piqued his Lordship, as to influence him shortly after in
disposing of all his Herefordshire property, part of which was
purchased by the trustees of Guy's Hospital, London.

CHAPTER VII.

CANONS, or Cannons, the estate of the Lake family, which had come into the Earl's possession by right of his first wife, is situated about a mile to the north of the little village of Edgware, Edgar, or Edgworth—(it is called and mentioned by all three names)—a place of undoubted antiquity, on the great Roman road known as Watling Street, and having many Roman remains in its vicinity.

The selection of this site for the Earl's mansion was deemed by many scarcely suitable for the magnificent structure proposed. To remedy, in a measure, its natural deficiencies, the Earl spent a large sum in changing the contour of the ground, accomplishing by art what nature had failed to create—an eligible site. Plans and estimates for the building were submitted by the best architects of those days; but whose were ultimately adopted it is impos-

sible to state; as during the erection of the
house, three well-known architects were employed, it is believed, in the following order,
viz. : Gibbs, James of Greenwich, and Sheppard.
The *Palladian* design was followed by all.
Though it may seem strange, it is, nevertheless, a
fact that no known plan, painting, drawing, or en-
graving, of the edifice *in toto* exists.   There are
elevations of the north and south fronts by
Hulsberg, dated respectively 1721 and 1730, but
these are only portions of the elevations purposed to be engraved; this is confirmed by the
latter date, as the building was finished some
years before 1730.   Strong, the mason who
undertook most of the stonework for St. Paul's
Cathedral and Blenheim, built the north front,
which its princely owner purposed should be
handed down, together with the whole building,
to posterity as a monument of his magnificence.
To this end, the foundations, 12 feet thick, were
reduced to 9 feet thick when above the ground
level.   The same substantial character applied to
everything connected with the edifice.   But,
alas! its grandeur scarcely survived its founder.
The exterior consisted of four sides, having
frontages to the north, south, east, and west, all
of freestone, and about 120 feet in length,

adorned with pilasters and columns of stone.
Surmounting each window was an antique head,
boldly sculptured; and along the top of each
front were life-size statues. The engravings,
just alluded to, depict but two sides; they have
led to conjecture as to whether the mansion
really possessed four sides of stone; or whether
these two made an imposing aspect from the
principal avenues, while the other two were
occupied simply by brick outbuildings. From
the absence of any drawing showing the four
fronts in detail, the latter assumption might
have some basis of truth. But the author,
after much research and piecing together various
scraps of information, is able to give an almost
complete description of the whole, though he
admits that at one time he almost despaired of
so doing. The account that follows will do much
to elucidate many hitherto vexed points, particularly one respecting the Earl's private chapel.
It has been stated that the private chapel was no
other than the present church of St. Lawrence,
Whitchurch, or Stanmore Parva, a gem little
known to Londoners, although within easy
access. Our transatlantic cousins, however, with
their usual keenness, have ferreted it out long
since, and it is much visited by them during the

holiday season. The belief that this church was
the Earl's private chapel will be shown to be
erroneous; while it is correct that the Earl had
the decorations of the church modelled after the
chapel at Canons, notably as regards the paintings
and the position of the organ.

The chief front of the residence at Canons
faced the east, and its avenue led directly to the
Church of St. Lawrence, Whitchurch, situate at
about half a mile's distance. The north front
faced the *parterre* and great canal, the west
the gardens, and the south looked over the space
occupied by the offices and stables, from which
ran another avenue. The principal entrance was
from the high road, about half a mile out of
Edgware, through a fine iron gate, with the
supporters of its noble owner on the pillar caps.
Inside the grounds were two neat lodges,[1]
modified later and inhabited by gentlemen, on
the estate being sold. The avenue to the mansion
was nearly a mile long and sufficiently wide to
allow three coaches to drive abreast. Half-way
between the lodges and the house was a large
basin of water, similar to those in Kensington
Gardens and Bushey Park. The approach was so
contrived as to face the angle of two sides of the

[1] Still to be seen.

ELEVATION OF THE SOUTH FRONT, CANONS.

Page 61

building, causing it to appear as one front from
the entrance gates. This illusion was heightened
by a turn given to the avenue before reaching
the mansion, this making, as it were, another
front appear, so that a person approaching
after following the contour of the avenue, saw
two fronts open to his view, whereas at first
he had seen but one. The visitor now found
himself at the east entrance, in front of a
large court which led to the salon and grand
staircase. To the left was another court,
leading to the back stairs, the latter as important as many so-called grand staircases.
The salon was supported by marble columns, and
decorated by Bellouchi, who also decorated the
ceiling of the grand staircase. The latter was
of marble, with steps in single blocks, some
twenty-two feet wide, and led to what were
termed the royal apartments, fronting the
parterre. The royal apartments consisted of a
suite of six noble rooms finely proportioned; the
plastering and gilding by Pergotti. The ceilings
were painted by Paulocci, and the doors [1] were
fitted with gold or silver furniture. All the
rooms were upholstered in the most sumptuous
manner. From these apartments, the earl's

[1] Probably silver gilt.

F

dressing room and library were approached, the latter facing the gardens. Here, another fine staircase, painted by Laguerre, and balustraded with wrought iron of a handsome design, descended into a court (that opened into the great area to the east), where the private chapel was situated on the right hand side and the kitchens on the left. The lower portion of the court was occupied by commodious and well designed stables.

The library was spacious, and was curiously adorned with books and statues, and a finely executed wood carving by Grinling Gibbons, representing " The stoning of Stephen." The chapel was prettily and neatly designed (here again Pergotti showed his skill in plaster and gilding) and contained a handsome altar. In an alcove above (the altar) was placed the organ by the celebrated Jordans; facing this, just over the entrance gates to the chapel (from the court. alluded to), was a spacious gallery for the Earl and his family, communicating by a door with the apartments above. A staircase descended from the gallery to the body of the chapel, in order to allow members of the family to approach the altar for the purposes of the sacrament, or other rites. The windows were

handsomely painted, the designs were taken from
the New Testament.

In the court that led to the east area was the
dining room, a spacious chamber containing a
handsome buffet, which displayed a service of
plate such as few sovereign princes could .boast.
At the end of the room was a small chamber,
where the musicians performed both vocal and
instrumental music during the repasts of the
family and guests.

The parterre, which faced the west, was
separated from the grand avenue and great court,
(that led to the principal staircase) by a handsome
iron balustrade. A similar railing was also used
to separate the mansion from the gardens on the
other side. The parterre was approached by a
long terrace walk which descended to it. On the
parterre was a row of gilded vases on pedestals,
down each side, so far as the great canal, where
it terminated. In the centre was a profusely
gilt statue of a gladiator, and the parterre was
further decorated by life-size statues. The canal
alluded to ran some distance through the grounds,
and is said to have been supplied with water from
springs at Stanmore, whence it was brought by
conduits.

The gardens were handsome and well stocked,

and are stated to have been designed by the well-known, but unfortunate, Alexander Blackwell. Their beauty was also increased by their being arranged in such a manner as to allow one to view the whole of them at once. This was accomplished by using iron balustrading to form the various divisions instead of walls or hedges. In the kitchen garden were some curious glass bee-hives.

Neat dwellings for the Earl's body-guard were at the end of the principal avenues. The body-guard consisted of eight men, drafted from old army sergeants in Chelsea Hospital, some of whom mounted guard over the mansion and grounds during the night, calling the hours and state of the weather, as the London watchmen used to do. On Sunday they preceded their noble patron to church, as halberdiers. Among the statues in the grounds were two, well known to scarce old Londoners of our day. For scores of years one of these graced, or disgraced, Leicester Square, that once howling wilderness before its improvement by Baron Grant; viz., the statue [1] of King George I., Chandos's royal and beneficent

[1] Wrongly stated in a recent publication on 'Leicester Square,' by John Holingshead, as having come from Canons, the seat of the Earl of Burlington! Also some query is advanced as to the date of its erection. The exact period will be found later.

LEICESTER SQUARE, SHOWING STATUE OF GEORGE I.

Page 68.

master. When in the park of Canons, it was handsomely gilt and awarded a prominent position. The
other is still to be seen in Golden Square, Regent
Street, and is that of his Majesty King George II.
For the Earl was privileged to live through four
reigns, viz., William and Mary, Anne, George I.,
and George II., receiving favours at the hands
of the last three sovereigns, more perhaps from
those of the Georges, as testified by his raising
their statues in his grounds.[1]

The foregoing description of the palace of
Canons is the most complete that has appeared in print for nearly 170 years, although
not all that will be brought before the reader
on this interesting subject; the remainder is
reserved until it shall appear in proper chrono-
logical sequence.

Though the Earl of Carnarvon had vacated
his appointment at the Pay Office, he was often
called upon to explain various unsettled matters
or cross references. A letter[1] sent on April
4th, 1715, to the Treasury shows the state of
the subsidies, and pay of the foreign troops,

---

[1] Readers of this volume might perchance like to acquaint
themselves with the exact position and surroundings of Canons;
a splendid photo relief map of North London, by the Rev. E.
McClure, M.A., and H. F. Brion (S.P.C.K., London, price 6d.),
will meet all requirements.

during the late war. In the preceding January,
a report[1] from Messrs. Foley and Harley,
Auditors of the Imprests, was presented on
the memorial of the Earl of Carnarvon, respecting
his payments to several regiments, on account of
their subsistence, clothing, pay, etc. The report
is minuted, 'prepare a privy seal.' Accordingly,
on the 4th of the following July, Mr. Harley
furnished a further report[1] on the state of the Earl
of Carnarvon's accounts, relating to the Army
in Flanders during 1710, which also could not be
passed (or allowed) without a privy seal. Again,
on the 28th of the same month, another memorial
was received from the Earl, respecting a sum of
799l. 12s. paid by a Mr. Whittingham for
recruits during 1708. The opinion expressed
was, that this amount should be allowed on the
paymaster's account of that year's land tax, then
devoted to army purposes.

On the 2nd of November[1] a minute was made
(on a document undated), termed the representation of Sir Bibye Lake, Bart., to the Lords of
the Treasury, in which he states that he paid into
the Exchequer 2257l. 4s. 10¼d., in part of
13,149l. 10s. 7½d. owing to the Crown, from
Robert Peters, late Receiver-General of Taxes for

[1] Redington's Calendar of Treasury Papers.

Hertfordshire. This is endorsed: Send to Earl Carnarvon and Sir Roger Mostyn, to know what has become of the South Sea stock that was to answer these assignments; in case it appears to be assigned to the trustees, then so much of the stock to be sold as will discharge the assignments, and, on the money being paid into the Exchequer on Peters' account, a warrant may then be issued for assigning the securities as desired.

These documents reveal that there were many matters unsettled in connection with the Earl's late appointment of Paymaster-General to the Forces abroad; in fact, they were not concluded until considerably later.

CHAPTER VIII.

Further reports on the Earl's late accounts as Paymaster
—Applications for Privy Seals—Petition of Robert
King re Peters—Copy of a Privy Seal for allowing certain accounts of the Earl whilst Paymaster—Gildon's
poem, termed "Canons, or the Vision," dedicated to
the Earl—The Earl still in favour at Court—Elected
Governor of the Turkey Company—Some particulars of
the Company.

DURING the year 1716, the Earl of Carnarvon was
fully occupied with the various matters in connection with his mansion at Canons, then in the
early stages of erection.

Mr. Auditor Harley[1] presented to the Lords of
the Treasury, on June 4th, 1716, a report on the
accounts of the Right Hon. James, Earl of Carnarvon, late Paymaster-General of the Forces in
Spain and Portugal, for the years 1710-11. Harley expresses an opinion in the report, that
Privy Seals were necessary for allowing the following expenditures :—

	£	s.	d.
To the German and Italian Forces serving in Spain during 1710	205,320	16	2
To the same for 1711	238,096	6	0

[1] Redington's Calendar of Treasury Papers.

	£	s.	d.
To Prince Eugene of Savoy in 1710 . .	4,047	1	3
To Count Gallosa in 1711	4,047	12	4½
To the Portuguese troops in Catalonia, 1710	103,100	10	0
To the Palatine troops in Catalonia, 1709-11	41,000	15	0
Ditto on account of extras	2,009	17	8
To the regiment of Grisons	12,527	19	0
For subsisting a Spanish regiment of Foot, and two troops of Horse, serving in Alicante during 1708	15,277	6	10½
To the regiment of Horse commanded by Major-General Hogan and Sir Daniel Carroll, respectively	16,267	12	1
For another commanded by the Marquis D'Orsa	19,386	5	6
To the Spanish regiment of Foot raised in Spain by the Earl of Galway . .	3,623	3	6
To Antonio Bellotiges and Joseph Louisa & Co. for supplying the Army in Spain with draughts, and mule carriage for Bread and Artillery trains, 1710 . .	109,321	13	9¾
To his Imperial Majesty on account of his subsidy as King of Spain for 1710 .	112,042	9	4½
And for 1711	37,970	19	3½
To the King of Portugal for maintaining 13,000 men for the year 1710 . .	150,000	0	0
For the year 1711	110,000	0	0

And some smaller items not worth giving in detail. This document is minuted, 'warrants to be prepared.'[1]

---

[1] There is some doubt as to whether the above accounts had not been brought up before Lord Wharton (when Privy Seal, 1714-15), who absolutely refused to seal them, whereupon they were adjourned. Upon his death, in 1715, they were again

Apropos to the matter mentioned in the last chapter *re* Peters, the following allusion is made in the Treasury papers [1] for this year, 1716, and appears under the form of a petition from Robert King (one of the sureties for Peters) to the House of Commons. The petition recites that he had laid his case, by several petitions, before the Lords of the Treasury, and thinks it very hard that he should be proceeded against by the Crown, having paid 2257*l*. 14*s*. 10½*d*. into the Exchequer. Likewise that the Crown had received 3007*l*. 11*s*. 3*d*., deposited in the Earl of Carnarvon's hands to pay the debt, and could receive the balance from Sir Robert Mostyn's office when the Lords of the Treasury order it to be paid.

The foregoing appears to refer to some irregularities in connection with the office of Receiver of Taxes for the County of Hertford. The guarantors of that official were called upon to make good certain misapplications by Peters.

laid before the new Lord Privy Seal, who, with the consent of the Treasury, finally passed them. These accounts were for the pay, etc., of the troops in Spain and Portugal, where it was impossible to procure such vouchers as the then course of the Exchequer required. But whether the figures were the same as previously recorded, cannot be proved with any certainty, though, after considering the matter carefully, the presumption is that they were.

[1] Redington's Calendar of Treasury Papers.

The sum of 3000*l*., said to be in the hands of the Earl of Carnarvon, may relate to the South Sea stock alluded to in a previous chapter, though it is not definitely stated.

Early in the year, 1717, application was again made for privy seals relative to the accounts of Earl of Carnarvon, when paymaster. To further these, a Sign Manual, dated April 12th, 1717, was issued, which ran as follows :—

"GEORGE R.[1]

"Whereas we are given to understand, that although the accounts of our right trusty and well-beloved cousin, James Earl of Carnarvon, for the time he continued Paymaster of the Forces acting in conjunction with the Allies, have been lately passed; yet by reason or neglect,[2] the several sums of money paid by him, which are hereunder particularized, and which were for services of the late war, have not been allowed him thereupon.

"Our will and pleasure therefore is, and we do hereby direct, authorize, and command, that in future accounts which the said earl shall or may render to you, or either of you, whilst he was

---

[1] From an original document in the Musgrave Collection, of MSS. relating to the Naval and Military affairs of the kingdom.

[2] Should be 'of neglect.'

paymaster of the said forces, to give allowance of the several sums following. Provided the payment of the said several sums do appear to you to be well and sufficiently vouched, and that no allowance of the said sums, or any part or parcel thereof, hath been before given to the said earl, upon any of his accounts already passed. That is to say—here follow 48 items amounting to 15,921*l*. 19*s*. 10¾*d*. Taking care to make proper certificate hereupon to the Commissioners for stating the Debts of the Army. And for so doing, this shall be to you, or either of you, a sufficient warrant.

" Given at our Court of St. James. The twelfth day of April, 1717.

" To our trusty and well-beloved Edward Harley and Thomas Foley, Auditors of our Imprests, and to all others it may concern."

The day preceding the issue of this Sign Manual, the auditors above named made a further report[1] to the Lords of the Treasury on the memorial of the Right Honourable James Earl of Carnarvon, upon the state, thereunto annexed, of several demands on the public, for pay, forage, mule money, and other services due to the general officers and others remaining unsatisfied.

[1] Redington's Calendar of Treasury Papers.

These claims accrued when Mr. Brydges was Paymaster-General of the Forces. The amount demanded was 6499*l.* 10*s.* 3¼*d.*, part of which, 2537*l.* 18*s.* 6¾*d.*, was for extraordinaries to foreign troops who served in Flanders, and for which no proofs had been produced. The balance was for other services during the same campaign. The report is not endorsed with any result of the treasurers' deliberations ; apparently quite unnecessary, or possibly included in the items, by issue of the Sign Manual.

Gildon dedicated a poem, entitled " Canons, or the Vision," to the Right Hon. James Earl of Carnarvon about this time. Why the poem was given this appellation it is hard to tell, nor does the preface assist in the elucidation of the matter. The preface consists of some ten pages, but no reference is made to the subject of the poem ; nor is it possible to glean much information from the introduction in verse, beginning as follows :—

> " While other arts, tho' of less rich a vein,
> From your large soul a just regard obtain,
> ¹ Bright *Pæans* son's presume you'll not refuse
> The nobler tribute of the Heaven-born muse."

And so on through four pages, when the poem itself opens thus:

¹ The meaning of this line is not clear in the original.

" Tired with the nauseous follies of the age,
    That busy fools and knaves so much engage,
    The thoughtless town I leave for shady groves,
    The ancient seat of true and harmless love."

The author then indulges in mythological rhapsodies for a score of pages, seemingly forgetting the title of his work. In fact, the only allusion made to Canons occurs in the following lines, intimating that the gods and goddesses had selected the site for the mansion :—

" Of chosen ' Canons,' with its groves and bowers,
    Its verdant lawns, its dales and gentle hills,
    Its standing lakes, and all its murmuring rills,
    Its sunny banks, and every shady glade,
    By consecrating hymns is sacred made."

This is enough to enable the reader to form an idea of the whole, without the infliction of a verbatim copy. The price of this effusion was certainly not prohibitive.[1] The poem contained almost the first allusion in verse to the noble Earl or to Canons : but such masters of verse as Pope and Young afterwards gave the Earl and his notable residence some attention. So closed the year 1717, not an eventful one for the Earl by any means, except that he managed to keep in good odour at Court.

[1] Published by J. Roberts, Warwick Lane, E.C. Price one shilling.

During February, 1718, the Earl of Carnarvon was unanimously elected Governor of the Turkey Company, in place of Sir Richard Onslow. The Earl's family connection had something to do with this appointment, as it has already been noticed that his father had been at one time the Company's Ambassador at the Porte; and the Earl's grandfather, on his mother's side, was a Turkey merchant of repute. The Turkey Company was originally established by Royal Charter, made perpetual by King James I., in 1605. It was not a joint stock company, like the East India, Greenland, and other really *bonâ-fide* monopolies, but merely a trading Company, under certain regulations for its management; nor were its members limited to place, or number, the membership being open to any subject of the realm free of the Company. The members on joining were supposed to contribute such proportionable sums as were necessary for the protection of the Company's trade. For many years, the Company was exempt from all monopolizing principles; any man paying a small fixed fee was admitted a member, and was then at liberty to trade to the Levant on his own account. The affairs of this corporation were managed by a governor and court of directors, for whose election every member, who had paid forty shillings Customs' duty the previous year, was entitled to vote, as well as upon all material questions concerning the Company. Their Charter empowered them to raise taxes from members; a privilege they exercised with great care. Nor did they permit their ambassadors and consuls abroad to levy arbitrary imposts on their trading members; the Company taxed the latter themselves, for necessary expenses, in furthering or protecting their commerce. Power was also given by their letters patent, with the approval of the Board of Trade, for the making of bye-laws for their own guidance. In fact, for a number of years, so good was their foundation and government, that an old authority states, "It has always been generously spoken of in opposition to others; being founded upon the inestimable liberty of trade, it prospered accordingly, and was extremely valuable to the Nation." The membership, about this period, consisted of some 800 merchants and others, residing in various parts of the kingdom and the Levant; the calling of Turkey merchant was then one of the most respectable for opulence and repute in the commercial world. The company also possessed a fleet of twenty ships armed with twenty-five or thirty guns each, trading to various ports in the Mediterranean. Besides appointing and paying an ambassador, secretary, physician, and consul to the ports, they had consuls, agents, dragomen, etc., at Smyrna, Aleppo, Alexandria, Algiers, Patmos, and other towns, at a cost of 15,000*l.* per annum. Two years before the Earl of Carnarvon's appointment as Governor, the Company had sent, as their ambassador to Constantinople, Edward Wortley Montague, Esq., husband of the celebrated Lady Mary Wortley Montague. The foregoing is a brief *résumé* of the constitution and character of the Corporation, in the management of which the Earl was elected to take an important part.

CHAPTER IX.

THE Earl, anxious to accomplish his desire to live in regal style, decided that the service in his private chapel should be worthy of its surroundings. He therefore retained at Canons a staff of the best vocal and instrumental artists. These were first placed under the direction of the celebrated Dr. John Christopher Pepusch, who was appointed Choir-master by the Earl, shortly after the Chapel was ready to be used for divine service. The decorations and other embellishments were not completed till later. The learned doctor retained his post for a short time, during which he composed the Morning and Evening Services, likewise a very fine *Magnificat*, and several anthems. But, for all this, the Earl was not content, desiring even greater things than the doctor could accomplish. At that time, George Frederic Handel was considered the greatest of composers, and had just been restored to court-favour by the influence of Handel's noble patron, the Earl of Burlington. Earl Carnarvon, therefore, determined that Handel should become the director of his music at Canons, and he was so appointed in 1718. Some chroniclers of Handel's career doubt whether he was employed by the Earl as a mere adjunct to the grandeur of Canons, or from motives of a superior kind. Sir John Hawkins, in his History of Music, considers it possible that the vocal and instrumental music, daily performed at Canons under Handel's direction, was superior in excellence to that enjoyed by any sovereign prince in Europe. This assertion is undoubtedly correct, judging from the still recognized merits of Handel's compositions. During Handel's sojourn at Canons (nearly two years), he composed for his noble patron several anthems, of which the best known are, *I will magnify thee; Let God arise! Have mercy on me; O come, let us sing; Sing unto the Lord; My song shall be always; As pants the hart; The Lord is my light; In the Lord put I my trust; O praise the Lord with one*

G 2

Consent; O praise the Lord, ye angels; also
other pieces, amongst them a fine *Te Deum.*
The latter is noticed in a curious MS.[1] note-
book, kept by Mr. Humfrey Wanley, librarian,
etc., to the Earl of Oxford, under the date of
May 15th, 1721. "Mr. Kaeyscht (at the Duke
of Chandos') has kindly promised to lend me the
score of Mr. Handel's *Te Deum,* being his second,
which he composed for the Duke of Chandos,
who can likewise procure the scores of all his
services and anthems."

Handel composed his Oratorio of *Esther* whilst
in the Earl's service; it is said to have been
composed upon the organ in the parish church of
St. Lawrence, Whitchurch. This may be correct,
for Handel is stated to have been the organist
at Whitchurch (though at this period—1718—
the Church was not ready for divine worship).
The Church was opened August, 1720, and the
previous fact confirms the existence of a private
chapel at Canons. Among the vocal performers
who assisted in rendering the Oratorio of
Esther, were Dr. Randall of Cambridge, and
Messrs. Brand and Savage, who, as boys, sang
in the Chorus. The Earl, as a mark of his
appreciation of the Oratorio, is stated to have

[1] Strawberry Hill Collection.

presented Handel with one thousand pounds.
Though now fully appreciated, Handel, even
when in the zenith of his fame, was not so
popular then as he is to-day. This assertion
may appear somewhat paradoxical, but the fact
is beyond doubt, and the assertion is borne out
by the following anecdote. While conducting
a morning concert at Leicester House—then
the residence of the widowed Princess of Wales,
to whose daughters he was music master,
when George III. was about four years of
age—Handel was so struck with the attention
the royal child paid to the music, that he ex-
claimed to the performers about him, " If that
young prince should live to ascend the throne,
then will be the era of Handel's glory." No
one will venture to say that his prophecy did not
find fulfilment. Previous to this the following
circumstance, which reveals the nervousness
or irritability of the great composer, occurred.
Though outwardly of an uncouth and robust
appearance, he suffered so much that he could
not bear to hear the tuning of musical instru-
ments; this was therefore always done before his
arrival in the orchestra. A musical wag, knowing his failing, and wanting a laugh at Handel's
expense, managed to gain access to the instru-

ments after the musicians having tuned, had left
them for a few minutes, at a performance when
H.R.H. the Prince of Wales was to be present, and unstrung them a half note or so lower
than the organ. On the arrival of the prince,
Handel gave the signal for the commencement of
the Oratorio, *cum spirito*, whereon a terrible
discord ensued. The enraged Conductor started
from his seat, overturning a double bass viol
which stood in his way, seized hold of a kettle-
drum, and threw it with such force at the head
of the leader of the band, that he lost his full-
bottomed wig with the exertion. Without stopping
to replace his wig, Handel strode to the front of
the orchestra, muttering vengeance, but so much
choked with choler, that distinct utterance was
denied him. In this ridiculous situation he stood
stamping and staring wildly about him for some
moments, whereat the whole audience was con-
vulsed with laughter, nor could he be prevailed
upon to resume his duties, until the prince went to
him and with great difficulty appeased his wrath.

The Earl of Carnarvon, having accepted the
Governorship of the Turkey Company, found
several grievances, in the form of departures
from its original proceedings, requiring adjust-
ment. The principal grievance was the imitating

of exclusive corporations who traded upon joint stock, without proper authority from Parliament by additional powers to their charter, and usurping this power by interdicting all trade in general to Turkey, insomuch that, for thirteen months—*circa* 1717—they had not suffered any woollen manufactures to be exported, Any of their members attempting to trade contrary to this prohibition, was mulcted in a fine of 20 per cent. duty upon his cloth, exacted and levied abroad, where no remedy could be obtained by this unfortunate trader. This procedure was such as no company, established by Parliament or Charter, had ventured to adopt, and the enactment appears all the more arbitrary when it is considered that the chief export to the Levant was cloth, of which commodity none had been permitted to be shipped there for thirteen months, with a possibility of its being restrained for another six, thus allowing an advantage to accrue to other nations who supplied the requirements of that market, and thereby carried away a large proportion of a staple industry of great consequence to this country. This was a somewhat complex matter for the Earl to handle. He, however, appears to have used his best endeavours to bring about an equitable arrangement.

The Turkey Company also enjoyed a portion
of the raw silk trade, as we see by the following extract from the "British Gazetteer" for
July 19th, 1718: "The Turkey Company have
received advice of their ships the *Duke of
Cambridge* and the *Dolphin,* as having arrived
in the Downs, having on board 900 bales of
silk."

During the year 1718, the Earl of Carnarvon
received further proofs of his Majesty's favour,
being nominated Master of the Horse in succession to Colonel Negus.

The Earl took steps at this period towards
acquiring a town residence, more suitable for
the owner of such a sumptuous edifice as Canons.
To this end he first decided on rebuilding
and enlarging his house in Albemarle Street,
and accordingly purchased the ground of his
own residence, and that of his late neighbour,
Sir William Wyndham. However, as he proceeded with this intention, he developed more
extravagant and magnificent ideas than the
space in Albemarle Street permitted him to
carry out. The site eventually selected will be
dealt with in a subsequent chapter.

Although the Earl was supposed to have
largely enriched himself during his tenure of

office as Paymaster, few, with such allegations
against him, even though legally unproved, have
ever enjoyed royal and public favour in so
marked a degree as this nobleman, for a period
extending over nearly three entire reigns. One
of the highest proofs of the royal favour was
the creation of the Earl, Marquis of Carnarvon
and Duke of Chandos, April, 1719. The official
announcement occurs in the *London Gazette*, No.
5742, and is incorrect by stating that the latter
dignity was in the county of Hertford—Hereford
being intended. As regards the noble peer's
continuance in public esteem, no doubt his
personal affability and generosity stood him in
better stead with the masses than any amount
of latter-day whitewashing would do. Another
circumstance worthy of mention occurred on
the 19th February, 1718. To Captain Henry
Rodney, of Walton-on-Thames, a son was born,
for whom he obtained permission of his Majesty
King George I., with that of the Earl of Carnarvon, to name *George*, after the first, and
Brydges after the latter. This favour Captain
Rodney was in a better position than many to
ask, being Commander of the royal yacht, which
frequently conveyed his Majesty, attended by
the Earl of Carnarvon, to or from Hanover.

The infant thus honoured with royal and noble
sponsors, went at an early age to Harrow
School, [1] where his noble godfather, the Earl,
had influence, being some time treasurer, or
one of its governors. He left school to enter
the Royal Navy at the age of twelve. This
youth became later the first Lord Rodney, one
of England's greatest naval heroes.

[1] The Duke of Chandos' first connection with Harrow School
was in 1713 ; when he was elected a Governor, in place of a
relation. He is credited with having introduced business
acumen and energy into the deliberations of that body ; as
well as ably seconding Mr. Brian the head master's labours,
to raise the status of the school. Success crowned their
efforts. From about 1721-1731, the Duke was acting trustee
of the school estate. His connection with the affairs of the
school did not cease till after 1740.

CHAPTER X.

THE Earl of Carnarvon having been "gazetted"
Duke of Chandos, only one other ceremony was
necessary for him to become entitled to all
privileges of his new rank. This was taking the
oath and his seat in the Lords. According to
the journals [1] of that time the Duke presented himself in his robes, introduced by their Graces of
Buckingham and Montague, with the usual
official attendance of Black Rod, Garter King
at Arms, and Lord Willoughby d'Eresby, who
officiated in the absence of the Lord Great
Chamberlain. His Grace of Chandos having
concluded the usual formalities, was placed on
the upper end of the Earls' bench. Hereafter
the Duke will be called by his new title, by

[1] Vol. xxi.

which he is much better known to latter-day
students and readers of history than as either the
Honourable James Brydges or Earl of Carnarvon.
The latter title was borne for many generations
by the Dormer family, till within a few years of
its being conferred on Mr. Brydges. Later, the
title of Duke became enlarged upon by his
compeers and the populace, who, to indicate
their perception of his munificence, prefixed
"Grand" or "Princely" to his ducal title.

The Duke's intention of building a new mansion in Albemarle Street was not carried out.
Having heard that the exiled Duke of Ormonde's
town house in St. James's Square had been sold
by the Commissioners of Inquiry to a Mr.
Hacket, an Irish attorney, for 7500*l*., he at once
instituted inquiries concerning it, with the result
that his Grace is mentioned as treating for its
purchase during May, 1719.

Lady Chandos, who had lived to see her son
attain the highest dignity in the peerage, was, on
the 23rd of May, 1719, taken dangerously ill at
her residence in Chapel Street, Westminster.
This illness, combined with her advanced age,
eighty years, caused much anxiety to her
relatives. Their fears were well founded;
she died on the 30th of that month. By

her death, an estate of 4000*l.* per annum passed to the Duke of Chandos. Lady Chandos is said to have told her family, on her death-bed, that she had little else to leave them ' except her blessing,' commending them to the care of their brother, the Duke. After the lying in state, then customary—a funeral in high life being a most elaborate and costly matter—her remains were taken by night into Herefordshire, and interred with other members of the Brydges family.

Soon after this event, his Grace concluded the purchase of the Duke of Ormonde's house in St. James's Square, but, before taking up his abode there, he had extensive structural alterations, as well as decorative repairs made.

The Duke of Chandos, true to those principles of magnificence which guided his life, built a yacht, a luxury which in those times very few noblemen possessed. The yacht was built at Greenwich, and thither he proceeded on Thursday, July 2nd, 1719, to witness its launching. It was christened the *Chandos*, and in honour of the event, the Duke gave a sum of 200*l.* to be distributed among the workmen. It is probable that the latest acquisition of his Grace was made rather for ostentation than for any real purpose, as no trace is to be found of the Duke's maritime exploits.

The Turkey Company received information, in July, 1719, of the capture by Spanish privateers, in the Straits of Gibraltar, of their ship the *Phœnix*, Captain Pallow, laden with raw hides, silk, and other commodities. This was one of the chances of war, a loss the more unfortunate, as the Company was in the bad graces of the trading community just then.

Canons, upon which large sums had been spent, was still unfinished in some respects, as we find by a notice in the *Weekly Journal*, August 18th, 1719, that "about a hundred tons of Portland stone was sent from London to Canons, to be used in the building of that structure." The Duke was maturing further plans for adding to the grandeur of his costly seat, having ground marked out for additions to its already fine porportions. Nor were the grounds forgotten by his Grace, who purposed taking in a mile of the by-road from Edgware to Bushey, for the purpose of cutting a fine canal. A Colonel Dobbins was of great service to the Duke in many of his transactions concerning Canons. Here again his Grace showed his appreciation of the axiom which he had

hitherto so well upheld, '*Noblesse oblige*,' for he
erected and presented to the gallant Colonel a
large house at Stanmore, as an acknowledgment
of the trouble he had taken in his Grace's behalf.

That the Duke still continued to reside in
Albemarle Street, when in town, is shown by a
communication he made to the Treasury from
thence, dated the 21st August, 1719, in connection with his late office of Paymaster, concerning some coals or accounts delivered to the
garrison at Gibraltar.

His Grace of Chandos was the eldest of a
family of twenty-two, though only seven survived infancy. These, on marrying, naturally
extended the collateral branches of the Chandos
family. Thus a Chronicle of those days states,
' that Lieut.-Colonel Jacobs, nephew of the
Duke of Chandos, of Lord Hinchingbroke's
regiment, has orders to sell his commission to
Colonel Price,' though the reason for this command is not given; nor does the following, which
appeared a week later, assist one in the elucidation, that Mr. Jacobs, nephew of the Duke of
Chandos, and brother of Colonel Jacobs, is
removed from his place of Deputy Comptroller at the Excise Office, and succeeded by

Mr. Hinman, a clerk in the same office, then receiving 80*l.* per annum. Whatever may have been the cause of these removals, they had no influence whatever upon public feeling towards the Duke, who, during August of this year, was elected one of the Governors of Christ's Hospital.

Although the Duke was certainly the most noted member of his family that had lived for some generations, neither Chandos nor Brydges Streets, in the west central district, are named after him, though Chandos Street, Cavendish Square, W., is. Chandos Street, W.C. was made *circa* 1637, and named after his ancestor William, Lord Chandos. Brydges Street, came into existence later (*circa* 1654) and is called after George Brydges, Lord Chandos. Another member of the family received a yet more regal affix than the subject of these pages, viz., Grey, fifth Lord Chandos, who from his magnificence was termed the " King of Cotswold." During the career of this nobleman the family Manor and Castle of Sudeley were at their best ; but these possessions passed away from the family in the third generation from the fifth Lord Chandos.

CHAPTER XI.

The Duke of Chandos and the New Mississippi Scheme—A short account of the undertaking—Anecdotes concerning Law and others—Matters relating to the Turkey Company —The Duke of Chandos attacked by highwaymen whilst coming to town from Canons.

His Grace of Chandos, though spending large sums in land-purchasing and building at this time, appears to have had ample means at command, enabling him to indulge in other schemes. He entered early into the affairs of the French Mississippi Company, and it is recorded[1] that, up to September of 1719, he had made 300,000*l.* by speculating in its stock. His Grace's agent for this matter was Mr. Moses Hart, who appears to have had good fortune himself, as he was then building a stately mansion at Isleworth (*Thistleworth*). The Mississippi Company, which found many supporters in England, and had as baneful an effect upon the people of France as the South Sea Scheme on the inhabitants of these islands, was contemporary with the latter pro-

[1] Original Weekly Journal, 1719.

H

ject. The French undertaking, however, was originated by a Scotchman, named John Law, of Lauriston. Law went to Paris in 1715, and procured an introduction to the Duke of Orleans, Regent during the minority of Louis XV. The Regent, being fond of men of vivacity and wit, was much pleased with Mr. Law, who possessed these qualities in a marked degree, and who was admitted soon after to the Council of the Regent. At this period France was groaning under the weight of debt incurred by the wars of the Great Monarch Louis XIV., which pressed heavily on all the community; the onerous taxes almost annihilating commercial industries. In fact, commerce and navigation had all but ceased to exist, merchants and traders were reduced to destitution, whilst the artisan was compelled to seek employment abroad. As a remedy for this deplorable condition of affairs, it was proposed to the Regent, to expunge at once all debts owing to the State by a National Bankruptcy. To this measure he had the good sense to object, though he gave countenance to a Commission, called the *Visa*, for examining into the claims of State creditors. Prior to the Committee being appointed, Mr. Law had approached the Regent with a scheme for remedying the state of affairs, by establishing a bank for issuing notes secured by landed property, as well as the whole of the Royal revenue; but the scheme was rejected. Mr. Law, nothing daunted, solicited and obtained letters patent, dated the 2nd and 21st of May, 1716, for establishing a private bank in Paris. The preamble in the charter of the 2nd May, however, recites the proposition orginally made to the Regent as regards the establishment of a Royal Bank. The capital for the bank of Law's, subscribed by him, his brother and a few friends, consisted of 1200 shares of 5000 livres each, i.e. about 250*l.* per share, thus forming an aggregate capital of 300,000*l.* sterling. The title adopted was "The General Bank of Law & Co.," which entered on its business under very favourable auspices, with high patronage and credit. The bank continued till the 4th of December, 1718, when the Regent, having noticed the advantages enjoyed by Law's Bank, whose paper the people were not adverse to accept, resolved to take the business into the hands of the Crown; a resolution but little relished by the astute Law and his associates. The public were informed that the Crown had

taken over Law's Bank, by paying out its proprietors, and becoming answerable for their
outstanding notes (amounting to fifty-nine millions of livres).   The title was then altered to that
of the " Royal Bank," and Mr. Law was made
Director-General.   Shortly after, branches were
opened at Lyons, La Rochelle, Tours, Orleans,
and Amiens.   The bank, under Royal auspices,
departed from the principles of commercial
credit that Mr. Law had fixed on in his undertaking, and proceeded on the lines of public
credit to further add to this evil, the tenour of
the notes was altered to " Payment at sight
in silver coin."   Mr. Law strenuously, but
unavailingly, opposed the alteration.   In the
February of 1720, the Royal Bank became
incorporated with " The Company of the Indies,"
or Mississippi Scheme, from which period to the
May following no less than 1,906,400,000 livres
were issued in paper, making with the fifty-nine
millions it was liable ·for (issued by Law's
General Bank) a total 2,696,000,000 livres.   Of
this extraordinary sum, 2,235,000,000 livres were
in circulation when the bank stopped payment on
the 29th May, 1720.   This hastened the down-
fall of the Mississippi Scheme, a project formed
by Mr. Law soon after the establishment of his

General Bank, and for awhile turned the heads
of the people of France, as well as attracted
the eyes of all Europe. Had this immense
project been carried out in entirety, it would
have placed France at a great advantage over
all other States. By the Scheme it was proposed to vest the whole possessions, effects,
and privileges of all the great trading companies, the farms, profits of the coinage, the
Royal and Government revenues, and the property
of the bank, in one powerful corporation, which,
having all the product of their affairs in its
hands, could have multiplied the circulation of
the paper currency to any desired extent. The
principle of this stupendous undertaking having
been approved by the Regent, steps for its establishment were taken, and letters patent granted,
during August, 1717. In these, the Corporation
was termed the Company of the West, and
granted the province of Louisiana, or the country
situate on the Mississippi. Its first issue was
200,000 shares of 500 livres each, payable in
'billets d'état,' at their face value. These were
at a great discount at this period, owing to the
irregular payments of interest, in fact so much so
that 500 livres 'billets' were worth little more than
150 livres in the open market, so that accepting

these at par was like effecting a loan to the Government of some 100,000,000 livres. Further issues of capital were made by the Company as its operations increased. The covetousness generated by the prospect of gain, through the operations of this Company was such as no nation had witnessed hitherto, and stimulated an excitement almost amounting to frenzy. The excitement prevailed to such an extent, that the whole four estates of the realm turned stock-jobbers, ultimately outbidding each other with such avidity, as to raise the price of the stock in November, 1717—(the month in which his Grace of Chandos is reported to have made a large sum by its sale) to 10,000 livres a 500 livres action (share). These purchases and sales of stock were first carried on in the Rue Quincampoix, to the great profit of the house owners there, until the space became too circumscribed, when the business was removed to the Place Vendôme, and ultimately to the Hôtel Soissons, which was bought from its owner by the Company at an enormous price. The fabulous rise in stock of the Company enabled many obscure persons to become millionaires. An army contractor, and a Madame de Chaumont made 127 millions of livres ; MM. de Vernie, de Farges and le Blanc 28 millions apiece ; and thousands of others obtained smaller sums. That many of these rapid acquirements occasioned much mirth the following will show. A lackey gained a fortune large enough to permit him to keep a chariot, but the first time he used it, from force of habit, he got up behind, in his old place, instead of inside ! Mr. Law's own coachman obtained a competency, and thereupon gave his master notice to quit. Law at first refused to release him, until he had procured as good a whip as himself to fill his place. To gain his freedom, Jehu gave his master the choice of two excellent coachmen, taking the rejected one into his own service.

With the mercurial rise of Mississippi stock Mr. Law reached the zenith of his fame, and had princes, dukes and lords, together with ladies of corresponding rank, in his ante-chamber, craving audiences. One day, at a more than usually crowded gathering of persons of the highest rank in France, waiting his pleasure for an interview, the Earl of Islay, afterwards Duke of Argyll, was announced by a servant, who was ordered to admit the Earl privately. On entering, he found Mr. Law writing what he surmised to be important letters, as he had observed

the number of people in the ante-room. But he
was greatly surprised and amused, when Mr. Law
informed him that he was merely giving instructions to his gardener, about "planting some
cabbages." Law sealed this important missive,
and proposed a game of picquet to his lordship,
who demurred, on the plea of inconveniencing
the many persons of rank who were waiting. To
this objection, Mr. Law replied, "Let them wait;
they do not come here out of personal regard for
me, only to plead for shares; so let them cool
their heels for an hour or so."

Mr. Law's wealth at this time cannot be exactly
estimated. It was asserted that he had lodged
twenty millions sterling in the Banks of England
and Amsterdam. But this appears to be fabulous.
On the other hand, it is true that he purchased no
less than fourteen estates, with titles of nobility
attached; his highest acquisition in this way
being the Marquisate of Rosny. In fact, Law's
resources at this period were so large that he
entered into negotiations for the purchase of the
celebrated 'Pitt' diamond, afterwards the chief
jewel in the regalia of France. But in the
midst of all his luxury, and in spite of the bad
character given him by many biographers, he did
not forget the poor, but gave large sums in alms;

he also assisted hospitals, and founded scholarships. At last (as in the case of the South Sea Bubble) an end came to this state of over inflation and false values, one of the immediate causes being a run on the bank, during which many were knocked down and trampled to death in the excitement to reach its counters. Mr. Law next came in for a share of the popular fury, the former idol being ruthlessly cast from his pedestal, and several attempts to lay violent hands on his person being made. At last his position became so untenable, that he fled to Brussels, on December 10th, 1720, where his wife soon after joined him, she having refused to depart from Paris until debts owing to various tradespeople had been discharged.

According to an authority on those times, Mr. Law had shown signs of mental derangement previous to the bursting of his 'Bubble' scheme. The same authority states, that "Law's head is so heated that he does not sleep; he gets out of bed almost every night, and runs stark staring mad about the room, making a terrible noise, sometimes singing and dancing, at other times swearing and staring. Some nights ago, his wife was forced to ring for persons to

---

[1] Hardwicke State Papers.

come to her assistance. The officer of Law's
guard, the first to answer the summons, found
Law, in his shirt, dancing round two chairs he
had placed in the middle of the room." After
travelling on the continent Mr. Law arrived in
London during October, 1721, and took up his
residence in Conduit Street, but soon after was
arraigned for slaying one Edward Wilson, in a
duel in 1694, although he had received the king's
pardon for the offence! Ultimately, the indictment
was quashed on the pardon being pleaded. Mr.
Law's means at this time are stated to have been
much reduced; decreased, no doubt, by his extravagant habits. However, he left the country
during 1722, lived at various places on the continent, and eventually died at Venice in 1729,
fifty-eight years of age, in poverty compared to his
former affluence. To the last he cherished hopes
of being recalled to France, though the death of
the Regent had made such an event almost impossible.

Thus the chimerical Mississippi Scheme was
sown, blossomed and died; an undertaking only
paralleled by the South Sea Bubble, though
the latter was insignificant as compared with
the audacious designs of the French Company.
But this would only be in accord with the latter-

day saying, "They manage these things better in France," whose people, even with the aid of the astute John Law, could not set aside the first principles of finance without disaster in the end. This subject has been dwelt on at some length, as the financial schemes of our Gallic neighbours, during the last century are not so well known to English readers as they might be.

Although the Turkey Company's export trade was at this period suffering by prohibitive measures framed by its Council, respecting the exportation of woollen cloths, the other branches appear to have been in a flourishing condition. The cargoes of two of their ships, which arrived in the Downs on September 9th of this year, 1719, were valued at 200,000*l*., and comprised amongst other goods, 329 bales of silk, 426 bags of gaulls, 51 bales of cotton yarn, 44 bales of grograin yarn, 272 bales of cotton wool, 2 chests of rhubarb, and 85 chests of soap.

The Duke of Chandos, desiring that his son, the Marquis of Carnarvon, should receive the benefit of a course of study at Oxford, entered him during November, 1719, at Balliol College, and placed him under the tuition of Mr. Hunt.

A nobleman of his Grace's exalted rank and

reputed wealth was not likely to be left unmo-
lested by the knights errant of the ' good old
times,' to wit, the highwaymen, whose polite
attentions were bestowed upon the Duke on
January 30th, 1720. Through the absence of
such an institution as the Central Press Association, at least three different versions of this affair
appeared in the daily papers. It is therefore
somewhat difficult to arrive at the exact circumstances, and recourse has been had to deduction,
by comparing the two accounts that agree on the
main points. The following account has therefore
been gathered.

As the Duke of Chandos was returning to town
from his seat at Canons, a lad hailed his Grace's
coach, saying that there were two highwaymen
waiting to attack it; whereon the Duke ordered
his servants, who, fortunately, were armed,
to seize them. This they accomplished, after a
chase as far as the vicinity of Paddington, then
a rural village. Upon his Grace coming up, he
was somewhat inclined to let the rogues go,
believing their purposed attack to be a drunken
freak, but some bystanders came forward and
urged that they were members of a gang that
infested the neighbourhood. The Duke thereupon ordered them to be bound and conveyed to

town. The miscreants were handed over to the authorities, and examined by Sir Thomas Clarges, who succeeded in getting them to inculpate several accomplices, some of whom were arrested next day, and committed to Newgate.

CHAPTER XII.

WHETHER the Duke of Chandos invested any of the gains made by speculating in Mississippi Stock in land, is not precisely known, though it is beyond dispute that, early in the year 1720, he acquired by purchase the manor of East Barnet [1] and also the neighbouring one of Totteridge, the purchases proving that his Grace was in possession of ample funds at this period. These he endeavoured to increase, like many others of both high and low degree just then, by dabbling in South Sea Stock. It is recorded that the Duke realized 30,000*l.* by this means during March of

---

[1] The manors of Friern Barnet, Kingsbury, Stanmore Magna Parva, likewise belonged to the Duke.

this year. Such a stroke of fortune appears to have led him, like many others, to increase his speculations, anticipating the same fortunate results ; but this was not realized.

His Grace was on friendly terms with many of the directors of the South Sea Company, particularly Sir Matthew Decker, to whom he presented his late town residence in Albemarle Street. Whether this was in return for favours shown, or for reasons of a friendly nature, cannot with any certainty be affirmed.

Extensive alterations were being carried out in the year 1720, at the Duke of Ormonde's late residence in St. James's Square, lately acquired by the Duke of Chandos. This mansion, Defoe terms " a noble palace, finely adorned by the Duke of Chandos." Its rental value was then said to be 300*l.* per annum. The repairs of a structural character, made by the Duke of Chandos, consisted in reflooring the entire premises, and demolishing and rebuilding the greater part of one side.

During the April of 1720, the Duke sold Queen Square, Westminster—(this site is now covered by Queen Anne's Mansions)—to a South Sea Company director, the well-known Sir Theodore Janssen or Jansen.

That the Duke of Chandos still had some connection with his late official appointment of Paymaster, the petition [1] of Captain Francis Stevens testifies. This document sets forth, that he was appointed by Sir Solomon de Medina, during 1711, to solicit and obtain for him several accounts for bread, etc., due during the late war, but having brought these matters to a satisfactory conclusion, Sir Solomon now refused to pay the sum agreed for his services. He therefore asked that this demand be adjusted out of the 2880*l.* in the hands of the Duke of Chandos, praying their lordships to order (the) petitioner's accounts to be laid before the Army Commissioners, and thus prevent his utter ruin. As may be presumed, their lordships refused to entertain this proposal, minuting the document on July 18th, 1720, to the effect that " This matter is not before my Lords." Now, whether the Duke of Chandos simply held the aforenamed sum as bailee on behalf of Sir Solomon, or still had the custody of certain disputed or unclaimed sums (the latter is improbable), cannot with absolute certainty be shown. However, it is clear that there was something connecting the Duke with his late office, or he would not

[1] Redington's Calendar of Treasury Papers.

have been cited by the petitioner in this matter.

The craze for speculation continued, and his Grace shared it in common with the populace and those of his own degree. His successes hitherto in such matters led him, about April or May, 1720, to enter heavily into South Sea Stock, his holding, some time in May, being worth, at the market price, about 300,000l. Anxious to obtain the best advice, he consulted a brother peer, the old Duke of Newcastle, who was supposed to possess considerable aptitude for business,[1] and asked him what he should do. The advice tendered, was "Sell forthwith." "No," replied Chandos, "I want half a million." "Then sell 100,000l. and take your chance for the rest," urged the shrewder peer. "No," said Chandos, "I'll keep it all, against its higher advance." He lost nearly all in the panic that shortly followed. In fact, it so happened that South Sea Stock had then all but reached its maximum price, though it never reached the inflated condition of its compeer, Mississippi Stock, which for a long time stood at 1800 per cent. premium; several transactions, in some of the frenzied moments of the supporters of that

[1] According to Grainger.

I

scheme, taking place at 2050 per cent.; while South Sea Stock never realized, for cash, the quoted 1000 per cent. premium.

Of the many satirical pamphlets, etc., published during the era of this mania, none make any direct allusion to the Duke of Chandos' speculations in South Sea securities. One, however, styled "Matter of Fact, or the Arraignment and Trial of the Directors of the South Sea Company," humorously describes a trial. One Councillor Crumbo (with his learned brothers Clamour, Query, and Trifle) appears to support the indictment, and leads off with the following rhapsody :—

> " When Stocks ran high and wits-production fell,
>   *Wit* grew a stock, which *wits* began to sell.
>   These taught, the ' Cits,' their birthright was to *cheat*,
>   That fortune could legitimate *deceit*."

> " Here, those that on him, menials joy'd to wait
>   With South Sea *squibs*, besiege a *Duke's* estate,
>   For *Cypher* scrolls, his rent-roll they command,
>   He gets their *paper*, and they get his *land*."

The latter allusion was probably intended for the Duke of Chandos, though it is doubtful whether the losses incurred by his speculations in stock of the South Sea Company shook

the Duke's fortune to the extent premised,
as soon after the collapse of this disastrous
scheme he purchased the whole of the north
side of Cavendish Square, then recently laid
out. Here he purposed to erect as noble a
mansion as any in London, considering his
then fine residence in St. James's Square not
sufficiently becoming the owner of 'Canons.'
Such an expenditure tends to prove that the
losses incurred by his speculations had not
during 1720 made such inroads on his Grace's
fortune as in any way to alter his mode of living.

Of the thousand and one schemes hatched in
'Change Alley during the 'Bubble' mania, many
well deserved the latter-day appellation of 'wild
cat.' In fact, the greater majority were little
better than webs spun by promoting spiders to
entrap those stupid flies, the 'British Public.'
A large number of these undertakings were so
utterly devoid of reason, that even our present
day race of 'gulls' would scarcely have been
deceived by any of them. Many had no legal
status whatever; others existed only in the
imagination of their promoters; but the populace were so reckless in their mania, that
permits to subscribe to an embryo company,
at some future time, were sold for as much

as 60*l.* All classes were bitten by the mania, even the Prince of Wales, who was announced as Chairman of the Welsh Copper Company. It must be admitted, that, taking the aristocracy as a body, they did not lend their names to, or become associated in the management of these enterprises, in the same ratio as their descendants have since done, under the present Limited Liability Acts. The subject of this work, however, stands out conspicuously as chairman of the York Buildings Company, whilst the Duke of Bridgewater appeared at the head of an undertaking for erecting houses in London and Westminster. The aggregate capital of the various schemes placed before the public during this period amounted to 300,000,000*l.*, an amount that then exceeded the value of all the land in the country.

The York Buildings Company, with which, to his loss, the Duke of Chandos was associated, was an old undertaking, incorporated in 1691, for supplying water from the Thames to the Strand and its neighbourhood. The works for this purpose were situated at the bottom of Buckingham Street, Strand, or upon some portion of the ground of York House. Here was erected, and worked for many years, one of the first practical

YORK BUILDINGS WATER WORKS, LONDON.

Page 116.

steam engines, the engine drawing water from the Thames at the rate of three tons a minute. This was accomplished by steam, which, arising from water in a copper boiler, became compressed and condensed, and then, moving by evaporation, struck a counterpoise. This struck another which moved a beam, thus imparting an up and down motion, thereby drawing water by means of a pump from the river, and raising through iron pipes to the top of a tower, where it was discharged into a great leaden cistern, and thence conveyed by pipes as far as Marylebone Fields. Here it was stored in a reservoir (now the centre of Cavendish Square), from which the then new houses in the neighbourhood, to the number of one thousand or more, were supplied. The description of this engine is compiled from an account that appeared *circa* 1729. So far, the York Buildings Company was a duly authorized undertaking, and continued its operations, with slight alterations, until the year 1719, when the proprietors sold their works for 7000*l.* to a syndicate, who set forth that they desired to improve them, and for this purpose invited subscriptions for new capital to the extent of 1,200,000*l.* The capital, however, was devoted to the purchasing of forfeited and other freehold estates; this ultimately brought the company almost to ruin. Such a departure from its original purpose would now be termed *ultra vires*, i.e., not provided for by the Articles of Association. It was at this period that the Duke of Chandos was elected Chairman of the Company, its new shares, for which 10*l.* had been paid, rising in agreement with the inflated condition of the market, to 305*l.*, or near 3000 per cent. premium. So far, all was smooth sailing, and his Grace evidently anticipated a 'boom'; though the satirists of that time portrayed this and similar speculations, on what was then a favourite vehicle for caricature, viz., a pack of cards. On the five of spades, runs the following doggerel :—

> "You that are blest with wealth by your Creator,
> And want to drown your money in Thames water,
> Buy but York Buildings, and the cistern there
> Will sink more pence than any fool can spare."

Unfortunately, the prognostication proved correct. The Company's stock, which had risen with its contemporaries to the price before stated, fell rapidly. This was brought about by the great progenitor of all these bubbles, the South Sea Company, which, by bringing legal authority to bear against the many unofficial undertakings,

soon laid this and similar institutions low.   The
writ of *scire facias*, issued on the petition of the
directors of the South Sea Company, expressly
mentions the York Buildings Company, the
Lustring Company, the Welsh Copper Company,
and the English Copper Company, and is supplemented by the ominous words " and divers
others, issued contrary to the law."   This action
on the part of the South Sea Company ultimately
recoiled on its own head, and it is by no means
certain that the momentary relief from the ma-
chinations of its rivals, secured by this means,
produced any material benefit to the South Sea
Company itself.   The instructions given to the
Crown lawyers on the issuing of the writ of *scire
facias*, were sufficient to strike terror into the
hearts of the unfortunate shareholders of the ille-
gitimate enterprises; the lawyers being instructed
to prosecute all who had opened books of subscription, together with those who had subscribed,
made, or accepted any transfer of stock in such.
This was indeed a drastic measure; it caused the
stock of the York Buildings Company to immediately fall from 300 to 200, and two days after
the commencement of proceedings, it was unsale-
able at any price whatever.   The same also
applies to the stock of the other companies

expressly mentioned. This was a disastrous matter to the shareholders, in common with the Duke of Chandos, who appears to have escaped the penalties mentioned in the writ, excepting the loss of his money. The York Buildings Company was afterwards reconstituted, and held lotteries, etc., for annuities; but his Grace retired from official connection with it. Thomas, Earl of Westmoreland, was afterwards appointed governor. The Company was one of the few that survived the South Sea mania, and it existed for some years into the present century.

CHAPTER XIII.

The Hon. and Rev. Henry Brydges, D.D.—The Duke of
Chandos' fortune after the losses in the 'Bubble'
year—His costly establishment at Canons—'Dr.' Thirlby
his Librarian—The parishioners of Whitchurch and the
Duke—He proposes to acquire a road from Canons to
Cavendish Square—Description of the intended new town
mansion—His Grace petitions the House of Lords on a
question of privilege—Committal of the offenders—
Their ultimate release upon payment of costs—He votes
against an inquiry into the affairs of the South Sea
Company—The Duke connects himself with the Royal
African Company.

THE Duke's brother, the Honourable and Rev.
Henry Brydges, D.D., having been alluded to
previously, opportunity is now taken to make
the reader better acquainted with him, particularly as he appears to have been the only other
member of the family who acquired distinction.
Mr. Brydges took his degree of D.D. upon his return from Aleppo, and settled down to minister
to the wants of his living, viz., the parishes of
Addlestrop and Broadwell, in Gloucestershire,
to which he was presented by his brother-in-law,

Theophilus Leigh, Esq., as early as 1699. In
the Convocation that met on April 9th, 1713, Dr.
Atterbury, Bishop of Rochester, then Prolo-
cutor, selected his old schoolfellow, Dr. Henry
Brydges, as his Vice. The Lower House, by a
unanimous vote, consented to the appointment ;
besides, a Vice was necessary, owing to the
frequent absence of Dr. Atterbury, who was
Chaplain to the Queen. Shortly after Dr.
Brydges was appointed Chaplain to his Majesty
King George I., a position he resigned in
1718, doubtless to the satisfaction of his friend,
Dr. Atterbury, who thereon appointed him
Archdeacon and Prebendary of Rochester in
1720, but whether his well-known intimacy with
Bishop Atterbury was a bar to his promotion to
a higher dignity in the Church is not definitely
recorded. However, upon the death of Prebendary Brabant in 1722, Dr. Brydges was given
the vacant stall in St. Paul's Cathedral. The
learned Doctor did not rise to any higher position
in the Church.

The losses sustained by the Duke, consequent
upon the fall in the stocks of the South Sea and
York Buildings Companies, led many to conjecture whether he could continue his princely style
of living at Canons. These surmises were, how-

ever, ill founded, the Duke continued to live as formerly. The establishment at Canons consisted of 120 persons, and was so ordered, that while there was an abundance for all, no waste should be allowed. With this end in view, Mr. Watts, an able accountant, had drawn out a plan by the Duke's orders, showing at a glance a day's, week's, or month's expenditure, upon a given annual income. The plan was engraved on a copper plate, and considered by many a very extraordinary effort of economical wisdom. His Grace sold all the fruit produced on the estate, not required for his own table, saying it was as much his property as the hay and corn off his fields. This remark was possibly made in reply to a suggestion that the fruit ought to be the gardeners' perquisite. It is doubtful whether anyone knew exactly what the Duke's resources were at this period; they, however, must have been of some magnitude, in spite of recent losses.

His Grace appointed as his Librarian at Canons the eccentric, but learned, ' Dr.' Thirlby—(Styan Thirlby), a well-known critic of the period, for whom, at one time, some degree of future eminence was presaged. These hopes, unfortunately, were frustrated by the Doctor's

quarrelsome temper, coupled with habits of in-
dolence, aggravated by an occasional too free
indulgence in alcoholic liquors. He first proceeded with studies for a clerical appointment,
but his eccentric and volatile nature induced him
to relinquish these suddenly, and apply himself
to the study of medicine. Tiring of medicine,
he adopted letters, ultimately accepting the care
of the Duke of Chandos' library at Canons.
During the time he held this office, he is said to
have displayed his erratic propensities to the
utmost, adopting a perverse and indolent inde-
pendence, and carrying this so far as to refuse
his company to his noble patron when solicited.
This, coupled with other vagaries, in time produced a rupture regretted by neither.

During the month of August, 1720, the internal
decorations of the parish church of St. Lawrence,
Whitchurch, were completed. The edifice, as
previously stated, had been rebuilt—except the
tower—by the Duke of Chandos. The parishioners, thinking his Grace would do more towards making their church worthy its proximity
to his noble mansion, sold the peal of bells,
anticipating that their patron would present
them with a larger and better set. Here their
judgment was at fault: the Duke, on hearing

what they had done, dashed their hopes to the
ground by refusing to comply with so strangely
expressed a demand. He, however, presented
them with handsome silver-gilt Communion
vessels. The church was re-opened for Divine
Service on the 29th August, 1720. Handel is
stated to have composed his Oratorio of *Esther*
for this occasion.[1]

His Grace's son, the Marquis of Carnarvon,
being on the eve of marriage, the Duke proposed
to settle his mansion in St. James's Square on
him. This, no doubt, was one of the reasons
for the erection of the proposed new residence
in Cavendish Square, particularly as the latter
position was best suited to another gigantic
project which his Grace had conceived. The
project was no less than the acquisition of
sufficient land to make a road (where he could
not procure any larger area), from his estate
of Canons to Cavendish Square; so that he
might be able to drive from one to the other
without passing out of his own possessions :
certainly a bold scheme, worthy of its originator,
though perhaps not then so unattainable as it
would be at the present time. Then, however,
the neighbourhood to the north and north-west

---

[1] See page 84.

of Cavendish Square was open country, in fact
the latter abutted on or was part of the old
Marylebone Fields. Had the Duke's speculations
in this memorable year been crowned with
success, he would most probably have set about
putting the idea into execution. Such a purpose
has been wrongly ascribed to his son, the second
Duke, who had not even the means, on his father's
death, to retain Canons as a residential estate,
and he could scarcely have wanted a private road
to an estate that was doomed to be deprived
of its mansion. The second Duke used his
steward's, or secretary's, residence on Brockley
Hill, adjacent to the estate of Canons, where
a room was handsomely fitted up to receive
his Grace when visiting Mr. Sharpe on business matters. The house on Brockley Hill was
adorned with several paintings, said to have
been part of King Charles's collection, but the
building has long since disappeared, and, as its
owner was not connected with the first Duke,
it is scarcely worth while to relate anything connected with it.

The intentions of the Duke of Chandos, re-
specting his proposed new residence in Cavendish
Square, are shown by an elevation designed by
John Price, in the King's Prints and Drawings,

British Museum. The style portrayed is similar to that of Canons, though scarcely on such an elaborate scale; but the proposed edifice was to have been of sufficient magnitude to cover almost the whole of the ground purchased by the Duke. However, the design was never carried out, although his Grace did eventually build on the ground at a later period and resided there.

On January 10th, 1721, the Duke of Chandos upheld his dignified character, by laying a complaint before the House of Lords [1] touching a breach of privilege committed by Samuel Burton, late Receiver of Taxes for the County of Radnor, and John Jones, late deputy Sheriff for the same county, in prosecuting a writ in his Majesty's Court of Exchequer (and by virtue of an *extant*) and other proceedings, entered the estate, and seized the goods and chattels of divers of his tenants, within the privilege of Parliament; and breach of the prerogatives of that House. This having been proved by several witnesses who were sworn and examined at the Bar of the House, it was ordered, " That in conformity with an Act passed the 12 and 13 Will. III. intituled, ' An Act for preventing any inconvenience that

[1] House of Lords Journal, vol. xxi.

may happen to privilege of Parliament,' that the Serjeant-at-Arms do forthwith attach the bodies of the said Samuel Burton and John Jones, and keep them in safe custody during the pleasure of this House." A fortnight later, the persons attached petitioned the House for their discharge: the petition was ordered to lie on the table. On the 1st of February, the Serjeant-at-Arms was ordered to bring the prisoners to the Bar of the House for examination, when, after hearing their evidence, they were adjudged guilty of the breach alleged, and ordered to remain in the custody of the Serjeant-at-Arms. John Jones remained in custody till the 28th of that month, when he was brought to the Bar of the House, received (when upon his knees) a reprimand from the Lord Chancellor, and was thereupon discharged on payment of his fees, these alone being no light matter. His fellow-prisoner, Samuel Burton, was kept in prison until the 7th of the following month, when he was brought up and discharged, having undergone a similar process.

About the middle of January, 1721, a debate took place in the Lords, relative to the expediency of an Inquiry into the frauds of the South Sea Company. After some discussion, the Inquiry was resolved upon by a majority of 22. The

Duke of Chandos [1] voted with the minority; his reason for so doing is difficult to define, unless it were to screen some personal friends connected with the Company.

With the infatuation of a gambler the Duke of Chandos now entered largely into another enterprise, viz., "The Royal African Company," [2] a Corporation that had borne a chequered career since the days of Elizabeth. In common with all joint stock undertakings this Company had enjoyed the advance in stocks during the Bubble mania of the preceding year, its shares, on which some 23*l.* had been paid, had risen to 200*l.*, but fell rapidly after the collapse of the South Sea Company, and rose again to par during January, 1721; this was brought about by the Company's determining (as they had many times before) to conduct their operations with spirit. To this end, permission was granted to increase their capital by the issue of new shares to the extent of 524,000*l.*; this sum was subscribed. A meeting was then held for the purpose of electing officers for the ensuing year, at the

[1] Egerton MSS.

[2] The Royal African Company, after existing for three centuries under various charters, died from impotence occasioned by mismanagement. Will latter-day Corporations show any better record !

K

offices of the Company in Leadenhall Street.   His
Majesty King George was elected Governor,
Francis Acton, Esq., Sub-governor, Sir Bibye Lake,
Bart., Deputy, and twenty-three gentlemen and
merchants, together with one peer (the Duke of
Chandos) as a Court of Assistants.   To his ultimate
cost his Grace subscribed largely for shares in this
Company, trusting, no doubt, to his own business
abilities, coupled with those of an influential body
of merchants on the Court to aid in recovering his
losses from the panic of the preceding year.   But
let the writer of a pamphlet concerning this Company at the time, tell the result of such a combined force of ' talent.'   " An eminent peer [1] was
made a director, ships were chartered, and laden
with goods and miners.   They fell a-trading and
digging through mountains in search of gold.
Their trading stock was soon spent, no gold was
found, and a great hole in the side of a hill alone
remains as an everlasting monument of their
industry."   Upon news being received of this
unfortunate state of affairs, the stock of the Company fell rapidly, touching 7 before the end of
the year.

[1] The Duke of Chandos.

CHAPTER XIV.

The Duke of Chandos elected a Governor of the Charterhouse
—The Marquis of Carnarvon receives the degree of LL.D.
—His Grace made reversionary Clerk of the Hanaper—
Account of that office—The Duke and the poet Gay—
Purchase of the Advowson of Rotherhithe by the Duke—
Departure of the Marquis of Carnarvon for " The Grand
Tour "—The Duke made Lord-Lieutenant of Hereford and
Radnor—Account of Sudeley Castle—His Grace's servant
waylaid on the road from Canons—The Duke made a Privy
Councillor—Honoured by the Prince of Wales with the
High Stewardship of Cantref Moelynaidd, Radnor—
Account of this manor—His Grace rewards a clergyman
for honesty—The Royal African Company again—Mr.
Speaker Onslow's character of the Duke.

CHAPTER XV.

THE Duke of Chandos received in 1721 another
proof of popularity, together with further marks
of royal favour. He was elected, early in April,
one of the Governors of the Charterhouse, in the
place of the late Duke of Buckingham.

On the 8th of April, the Marquis of Carnarvon
received the degree of LL.D. at Oxford. His
lordship's tutor, a Mr. Stewart, took that of
M.D. at the same time.

One of the favours bestowed upon his Grace at

this period by his Majesty King George II. was his
nomination as reversionary Clerk of the Hanaper
(or Hamper) in which grant he managed to get his
sons John (Marquis of Carnarvon) and Henry included. As many may be curious to know what
this office was, the following account, compiled
from a curious old work dated 1727, giving the
nature and business of the several public offices,
will be interesting. . The Clerk of the Hanaper
was an Officer of Chancery, sometimes termed
Warden of the Hamper; his duty was to receive
all money due to the Crown for seals on charters,
patents, writs, &c., together with the fees to the
officers for examining and enrolling the same.
He was further obliged to attend the Lord
Chancellor daily, in term time, and at all times
of sealing, having with him leather bags wherein to place the documents sealed. These bags
were then closed and impressed with the Lord
Chancellor's private seal, and delivered to the
Comptroller of the Hanaper, who attended on
seal days, to check and enter all documents enclosed in them, comparing these with the Clerk
of the Hanaper's account. It is not to be
assumed that a nobleman of his Grace's position
did any drudgery of office, as stated; this was
done no doubt by a deputy. The emoluments,

on the other hand, were received by the Duke, his substitute getting a moderate remuneration.

Gay, the poet, who had been a great sufferer by the decline in South Sea Stock because he had not sold when advised, ventured amongst the shoals of 'Finance,' beginning by accepting a present of 1000*l*. of South Sea Stock from the 'Elder' Craggs. He was induced this year, as some *solatium* to his losses, to publish his poems by subscription, and was so fortunate as to obtain much encouragement. Their Royal Highnesses the Prince and Princess of Wales sent their names as subscribers for a handsome amount. Among the most liberal of the poet's patrons were the Duke of Chandos and the Earl of Burlington; each took fifty copies of the book. A few such subscribers nowadays would ensure the success of any limited edition.

The Duke about this time purchased (possibly with a view to providing a friend or relative with a 'living'), from Edmund Stokes and others, the advowson of Rotherhithe, a parish then more rural and inviting than now.

The education of his Grace's son and heir would not have been deemed complete in those times without his making the 'Grand Tour.' The Marquis set out during July, 1721. Gossip was

then as rife as it is at present concerning the probable or projected marriages of persons of rank.
In this case his lordship was supposed to be
going to marry Lady Anne Egerton, only daughter
of the Duke of Bridgewater, on his return from
abroad; but the rumour was only a further proof
of the old adage: " That common report is—"
well, a common perverter of the truth.

However unfortunate the Duke had been during
the past year in his financial speculations, his
star was still in the ascendant at Court, as in
August, 1721, he received from the King the
Lord-Lieutenancies of the Counties of Hereford
and Radnor, in place of Earl Coningsby deceased. His Grace much appreciated his Majesty's kindness; Herefordshire was his native
county, and its capital town had been represented by him in Parliament for many years. It
had also associations of another kind, though the
bulk of the estates appertaining to the Barony
of Chandos lay in Gloucestershire. The sixth
Lord left the Manor and Castle of Sudeley to his
wife Jane, daughter of Lord Rivers, who survived
him. She married George Pitt, Esq., of Strathfield
Saye, Hampshire, for her second husband, and
by this means the ancestral titular estate of the
Chandos family passed away from it. Sudeley

Castle is of great historic interest; Queen
Catherine Parr died there, September 5th, 1548,
and was buried in the chapel adjoining the
castle. Her funeral is memorable from the fact
that it was the first royal interment according to
the rites of the Reformed Church. Queen Elizabeth visited Sudeley Castle in 1592, and here
Grey, the fifth Lord, already alluded to as the
'King of Cotswold,' held his 'Court' in great
splendour. During the Parliamentary War,
in 1642, this castle sustained a siege, on behalf
of the King, who visited it the following year.
Upon its being surrendered to the forces of
Parliament, 'Old Noll's' troopers of the
'Praise God Barebones' sort desecrated the
chapel; many monuments appertaining to the
Chandos family were ruthlessly destroyed, and
the graves violated. This closed the career of
the Castle as a stronghold and complete edifice;
—such it had been since the days of Stephen—its
walls soon after fell into decay.

In 1802, Pitt Rivers, Esq., a descendant of the
before mentioned George Pitt, Esq., was created
Baron Rivers of Sudeley Castle, Gloucester,
though some considered that the older Barony[1] of

[1] See Sir Samuel Egerton Brydges, Bart., "*Lex terræ*," 1831:
also G. F. Beltz " Review of the Chandos Peerage Case," for the
context.

Chandos was not extinct. Baron Rivers disposed of the ruins of the castle, together with fifty or sixty acres of land, to Richard, Marquis of Buckingham and Chandos, grandfather of the late Duke of Buckingham and Chandos, created in 1822. This nobleman sold the castle and land to John and William Dent, who had acquired nearly all the estate belonging to the ancient Manor of Sudeley, in 1837. Under their ownership the north quadrangle was restored, and other improvements were effected.

On a Sunday evening in September of this year, one of the Duke's servants was returning to town from Canons on horseback, when his horse fell, unseating its rider ; whereupon two footpads attacked him, and, before he could regain his feet, robbed him of his whip and about five shillings. It is a matter of some surprise that these attacks were not more frequent on the Duke or his retinue, the 'vulgar folk' having acquired a most extravagant idea of the amount of his Grace's wealth. But it is probable that the Duke's magnanimous and benevolent nature had gained respect even amongst these enemies of law and order.

The year now under review was almost literally crammed with honours for the

'Princely' Chandos. He received proofs still further of his Majesty's goodwill, being appointed a member of his Privy Council. The Prince of Wales followed his august father's example by appointing his Grace, during November, High Steward of Cantemelenis, Radnor—(this is the 'press' rendering of the name—"Cantref Moelynaidd" [1] its correct appellation)—is an ancient and extensive tract of country, which was governed in early times by chieftains styling themselves Lords of Ffenllys and Moelynaidd, some of whom became Kings of Britain, others Dukes and Earls of Cornwall. William Rufus put an end to this long chain of succession by granting the territory to Ralph de Mortimer. Its conquest was not so easy a matter as its grant, for it was not accomplished until the reign of Edward I., who confirmed the grant to the family of Mortimer, in the person of Earl Wigmore. The Earl was found guilty of treason, the grant then escheated to the Crown, but was re-granted to the same earldom, *temp.* Edward II. On the failure of the male line of this family, it again passed into the ownership of the Crown by the marriage of Anne, heiress of the Mortimers, with Richard, Duke of York, whose

[1] Williams's Radnor.

son became Edward IV., and has been so held
to latter days. This vast estate at one time
contained one hundred townships, the tenants
faithfully paying their rents into the Royal
Treasury by the hands of receivers, till the
twelfth year of Charles the First's reign, when
Stewards, or High Stewards, as they style
themselves, were appointed. The first Steward
was the Earl of Pembroke and Montgomery. Among other notable persons who
have held this honour are such names as
the Marquis of Powis, Sir Robert, and Mr.
Harley, until the name of his Grace of
Chandos is reached—(6th Geo. I). The appointment was given to the Duke on the 4th
of February, 1721, though chronicles of those
times (in the form of newspaper reports),
mostly fail to inform their readers until the
following December. There were many customs
attached to the office of Steward, one being
authority to hold a Court Baron every three
weeks. In one sense, the preliminary value of
the appointment was not large, it amounted to
6l. 13s. 4d. per annum; this, however, was
supplemented by fees from the different Courts
which the Steward was empowered to hold
(chiefly for election purposes). But perhaps its

most important and profitable privilege was
that of the free and several fisheries together
with the rights of hawking and hunting, with
full power to depute these rights to others. The
'Grand' Duke held the office for twenty-three
years, in fact, until his decease, but since the
days of George III. the estate has been leased
principally to members of the Harley family.

The many signs of royal regard bestowed upon
his Grace, led the disseminators of news, in 1722,
to prognosticate further favours; it was reported
during the month of May that the Duke was to
receive one of the vacant garters. In this attempt
to forecast the bestowal of their sovereign's goodness, they were not happy, as his Grace did not
receive one of the vacant stalls in St. George's
Chapel.

The terror that had been struck into many
promoters of, and investors in, unauthorized joint
stock companies before the panic of 1720, by
the Government directing a prosecution against
them, was lessened in a measure this year, 1722;
the Governor of the English Copper Company
informing its shareholders at a Court held during
June, that upon their petition a *nolle prosequi*
had been entered by the Attorney-General on the
writ of *scire facias*, in which this Company was

specially named. As two of the other Companies
out of the four originally endorsed on this writ
were still continuing business, viz.: the York
Buildings and English Lustring Companies, it is
probable that they had satisfied the ends of
justice, receiving tacit or implied permission to
continue their operations, though no doubt in a
modified form.

A clergyman, whom his Grace much esteemed,
was at Canons one day, looking over the library.
The Duke, wishing to make the divine a present,
as a small token of his esteem, desired him
to select any book he liked. The learned
divine thereon chose a volume of no great
value. On reaching home, and opening the book,
he was greatly surprised to find a bank bill of
considerable value between its pages. Feeling
sure that his Grace could not possibly have been
aware of the likelihood of his choosing the work
in question, he hastened to Canons the next day,
with both book and bill, and placed them before
the Duke, who thanked him for his trouble,
and took back the note or bill, only to exchange
it, however, for one of double the value. This
he handed to his clerical friend, remarking,
"Accept that, sir, for your honesty." This cir-

[1] Grainger's Biography.

cumstance is quite in harmony with the character of the Duke.

That fickle jade fortune further distressed the 'Princely' Chandos this year. Anxious, no doubt, to retrieve his previous losses in joint stock undertakings, he wooed the goddess somewhat too ardently, with the usual result to those who have too much zeal; she proved a 'jilt.' This was fully exemplified by the unfortunate turn taken by the affairs of the Royal African Company. Its directors made a call of 5l. a share, and shortly after ruthlessly declared a reduced dividend of 1½ per cent. These combined circumstances did not tend to improve a falling market. The call pressed heavily on several large holders of the Company's Stock; their shares, with 23l. paid, being then only worth 7l. The Duke is said to have behaved in his usual magnanimous manner, sticking to the 'ship,' with great loss ultimately to himself and his family.

Speaker Onslow's allusions to the Duke's career may not be out of place here, although in one or two instances the terms used scarcely seem warranted. "The Duke of Chandos was the most surprising instance of a change of fortune raised by a man himself, that had happened,

I believe, in any age. When he first entered into the office of Paymaster, he had little or no estate of his own, and never inherited more than a few hundred pounds per annum;[1] but by the means of this office, and the improvements of money, in little more than ten years, living expensively too in the meanwhile, he had accumulated a fortune of six or seven hundred thousand pounds—I have heard more—and without any vices, or being addicted to pleasures, in the compass of twenty-five years he was reduced to almost the difficulties of indigence,[2] by a course of extravagance in his expenditure that had neither taste, use, or sense in them. He was a bubble for every project, and a dupe to men that nobody else would[3] keep company with. Yet with all this, he had parts of understanding and knowledge, experience of men and business and a gravity of deportment, which more qualified him for a wise man, than what the wisest men have generally been possessed with. He fell— for so indeed it should be called—pitied and lamented by all who knew him, for a man of more true goodness of nature, or gentleness of manners

[1] Doubtful.

[2] This is a rather strong term, but the reader will be able to judge for himself as he proceeds.

[3] I cannot entirely substantiate this.—AUTHOR.

never lived." The foregoing character confirms
that of other authorities, although Speaker Onslow
furnishes details which many have overlooked;
these will assist in elucidating much that will
appear in the following pages.

CHAPTER XV.

THE Duke of Chandos, though a kind master and generous patron, possessed a shrewd knowledge of men, gained by business intercourse with their varied ranks, which would have served him well if carried into all his transactions, and particularly money matters. As an instance of his perspicuity, the following is recorded. The Duke, in his occasional bounties to labourers on his estate, would never exceed the sum of sixpence to each; this, being personally given, was generally accompanied by, "That may do you good, more, idle and drunk," a sweeping allegation, though it contains a substratum of truth.

The immortal author of "Robinson Crusoe," Daniel Defoe, in his work entitled "A Gentle-

man's Tour through England," published in 1724,
refers to the magnificence of Canons, but he does
not give so precise an account as that already
presented to the reader. He, however, frankly
acknowledges that " his pen could ill describe the
place, a pencil not much better, being only fit to
be spoken of when on the spot." After other
panegyrics, the observant Defoe dwells rapturously
upon the private chapel, and further dwells on the
rapidity with which the whole edifice was erected,
and thinks its noble owner fully deserving of the
motto assumed by one of the French Kings,
"He saw and it was made." The retinue of his
Grace, he avers, numbered some 120 persons
(thus bearing out previous allusions); the cater-
ing for these being conducted so that " a face of
plenty appears in every part of it, nothing need-
ful being withheld, nothing pleasant restrained,
every servant in the house is made easy, and his
life comfortable, and they have the felicity that
it is their lord's delight and desire it should be
so." Defoe's visit took place April, 1724, as he
mentions finding the family much pleased by the
marriage of the Duke's eldest son, John, Marquis
of Carnarvon, who married, early in this month,
the Lady Catherine Tollemache, daughter of the
Earl of Dysart, the ceremony taking place at
Canons.

L

His Grace still maintained the services in his private chapel at Canons; although they were not conducted by such contemporary geniuses as Handel or Dr. Pepusch. A newspaper of that period states, that a Mr. Munroe followed those great masters; this gentleman had previously served his Grace in the less dignified position of page, and afterwards was appointed his organist. Mr. Munroe no doubt possessed musical talent; for during the same year he was appointed organist of St. Peter's, Cornhill.

The question of privilege that the Duke of Chandos had raised some few years previously in the Lords, was again brought before their Lordships by his Grace, in another form, on the 15th March, 1725. The breach complained of was the arrest of one Richard Leach, a helper in the stables of James, Duke of Chandos, by one Timothy King, an officer of the Marshalsea Court, at the suit of Edward Brignall, during the sitting of their Honourable House, in other words, during the Sessions of Parliament. Having heard the evidence in support of the breach, the Gentleman Usher of the Black Rod, his deputy or deputies, were ordered to attach the persons of the aforesaid Timothy King and Edward Brignall, for the offence alleged, and to hold them in safe custody during the pleasure of that House. This having been accomplished, they were brought to the Bar of the House, in custody of the Gentleman Usher of the Black Rod, where, upon their knees, they received a reprimand for their offence from the Lord Chancellor, and thereon were ordered to be discharged from custody, upon payment of certain fees (these had been recently re-adjusted).

	£	s.	d.
To the Gentleman Usher of the Black Rod (on attachment	5	0	0
Ditto upon discharge	5	0	0
For every day's custody	1	6	8
To the Yeoman Usher, on attachment . . .	2	0	0
Ditto upon discharge	2	0	0
To the Clerk of the Parliament for the order of release	6	13	4
To his Clerk Assistant	2	0	0

Verily a merry little scale of fees, wherefrom to frame a nice little bill for an unfortunate delinquent enjoying the appellation "commoner." On the other hand, the peers were heavily mulcted if their transgressions needed the services of the Gentleman Usher.

The reader has had an account of Canons and its grounds; mention is now to be made of its art treasures. The observant George Vertue,[1]— the famous engraver and connoisseur—alludes

---

[1] Strawberry Hill MSS.

to them after a visit to Canons, *circa* 1725, in these words : "The Duke of Chandos' house, several paintings in the chapel by Bellouchi, in the house some by Sir James Thornhill, much fine sculpture, marble statues, books, etc. The great grandfather (picture) of the Duke, an old man, the face very natural—the manner stiff. The Duke's father, a wig and whiskers ; his grandfather, a half-length Vandyck, a good copy ; several of his relations, and his own picture ; his first lady, his son, and a daughter, by Sir Godfrey Kneller ; the Duchess of Buckingham in a black setting, with children by her ; the Duke's picture hung up above, supposed to have been painted after his death, either by Vandyck or after him, most likely Mytens. At Whitchurch, near Canons. The Church built lately, of brick, and adorned at the expense of the Duke of Chandos ; the altar painted by Laguerre ; the ceiling, eight Scripture scenes, the life of Christ ; two other large pieces by the altar, all ornamented, and painted by the same master with great force and strength. A nativity and a dead Christ, since painted by side of altar, by another hand, Bellouchi, an Italian." The foregoing is but a meagre account of the pictures and treasures at Canons, but important

as concerning the paintings in the parish church.
Vertue, after the Duke's death, made a further
inspection of the objects of art, particularly the
pictures, during their disposal; his remarks,
together with a full account of the paintings,
will be given later.[1]

The summer of 1725 was particularly wet, and
seriously affected the hay harvest; so much
so as to cause great distress among those who
had journeyed in search of hay-making. Towards the end of June three hundred of these
persons marched to the Royal Exchange, where
a collection was made for them amongst the
merchants. The amount, being divided, came to
about sixpence each. The Duke, having heard of
the circumstance, considered it a good opportunity
for his appearance as the Princely Chandos, and
caused it to be intimated that, if any necessitous
husbandmen were in the neighbourhood of Canons,
and would present themselves at his gates on a
certain day, they should be relieved. To this
invitation about one hundred and fifty assembled,
when each was given a half crown and a sixpenny
loaf. It is said such kindness led many of the
neighbouring gentry to follow the Duke's example.

[1] See pages 213—219.

The disastrous agricultural season alluded to and the affairs of the African Company, appear to have made inroads upon his Grace's fortune this year, as the following letter [1] shows :—

"Canons,

"October 16th, 1725.

"My Lord,—The convincing proof you have been pleased to give me of your wishes for ye welfare of my family [2] (ye happiness of which you have in so distinguished a manner been so good to compleat) makes me flatter myself you will not take amiss ye liberty I use to communicate to you, a matter of some importance to Lord Carnarvon, upon which I shall be proud to know your Lordship's sentiments, and to receive ye honour of your advice. It relates my Lord to ye grant of Enfield Chace, made by King William and Queen Mary to Sir Robert Howard, and which I bought of Sir William Pearson, some years ago. I have in it a term of fifty-three years, to commence from ye expiration of that made to Lord Lisburn, by King James, in which Mr. Pepper, who is now in possession of it, hath still twelve years to run; this gentleman finding himself not so well able

[1] Original in MS. Department, British Museum.
[2] Referring to the marriage of his son with the Earl of Dysart's daughter.

through ye decay of his health, to take that care
of it, it requires, is inclined to dispose of ye
remainder of his term. Mr. Pulteney having it
applied to me to know if in case he could agree
with him I would be willing to sell him likewise
my grant, by which means he would be secured,
of a term of sixty-eight years. I cannot but
acknowledge I inadvertently gave him too much
encouragement to proceed in such a treaty, which
hath had that effect, that he now acquaints me he
hath absolutely concluded it with ye Government,
for a sum certain, but as I have since considered
more carefully ye importance of this grant, from
ye severall advantages which may arise from it,
I think it is of too great consequence to be
parted with rashly, from my family, and Mr.
Pulteney is so sensible of this, that he generously
offers that in case I incline to keep it, to relinquish his bargain with Mr. Pepper to me, upon
ye terms ye hath agreed it. By ye particulars
which I have ye honour to enclose to you, your
Lordship will see—for it is upwards of 630*l*. per
annum—but the great advantage which may be
hoped for in time from it consists chiefly in this,
that ye Chais—Chace—contains 14,000 acres, most
of which will let for between 20*s*. and 30*s*. an
acre. If not and ye publick should be inclined

to enclose this ground there is no doubt, but a large tract thereof would be assigned to ye owner of this grant, in consideration of his right or if that design — which hath been often of late thought on—should now be effective, it is to be hoped, and I think hardly to be questioned, but that Lord Carnarvon would find it almost enough to obtain lycenzes—licences—from time to time, to enclose portions of it. Mr. Pepper hath lately had leave to do so, by ninety odd acres, and if it was granted to him Lord Carnarvon, will have no reason to despair, of getting ye same liberty to do ye like, by more considerable parcels. I might add it is not distant above seven miles from Canons, hath an extraordinary good house upon it, fit for a gentleman, gardens well planted, with fruit, and several good fish ponds. It joyns likewise to ye Manor of Totteridge, and Barnet which your lordship knows are settled on your son-in-law (Lord Canarvon). I can sell my grant for between eight and ten thousand pounds, but as I should be concerned for so fine an estate, and so desirable—With regard to ye command as well as profit it carries with it—go out of my family. What I have humbly to propose to your lordship, is, that if you think it a matter so far worthy your notice so to incline ye to lay down ye money

Mr. Pulteney, hath agreed to give Mr. Pepper
—which I take to be between four and five
thousand pounds—and 4000*l.* more to me for my
grant I'll assign it over to Lord Carnarvon, and
consent to it being settled in jointure, on his lady,
and will pay your lordship interest at ye rate of
4 per cent. for ye 4000*l.*, ye amount of ye purchase,
ye make of my grant, and question not but Lord
Carnarvon will do ye same for ye money, you
shall be pleased to lay down for Mr. Pulteney,
for what he is to pay Mr. Pepper for ye remainder
of his term, by this means your lordship will have
an opportunity of increasing ye favours ye have
already bestowed upon me by augmenting Lord
Carnarvon's present estate, and your daughters
joynture, above 630*l.* per annum—and which in
all probability will come in time to be a great deal
more—without being out of pocket yourself, since
your having to receive interest, for ye money, you
lay down, renders this transaction, little other
than changing hands, in a mortgage, especially
since, you are both very ready and desirous to
consent that this estate, be charged with and
made a security, for ye money to be disposed of
by your lordship, as you shall think fit. I am
sensible my Lord it will be troublesome for you
to write an answer to this long letter and there-

fore, if you'll allow me ye liberty I'll have ye
honor, to wait on you on Tuesday morning to
know your pleasure herein, and ye other business.
I have promised Mr. Pulteney to let him know what
he is to depend on in this affair ye middle of next
week. Lord and Lady Carnarvon desires Lady
Dysart, and your Lordship will please to accept
of their most humble duties, and my wife joyns
with me, in ye same assurances on her part, that
I do on mine, that I am to her Ladyship and to
your Lordship,

"My Lord,

" A most faithfull and obedient Servant,

" Chandos."

This letter is a very fine specimen of 'special
pleading' in the epistolary art, as well as a
proof that the rumours afloat were correct;
though his Grace still resided at Canons, and
kept up his residences at Bath and elsewhere. It
cannot be said with certainty, that Lord Dysart
complied with his noble relative's request; it is
thought he did not, and other references tend to
confirm this.

CHAPTER XVI.

John, Marquis of Carnarvon, enters the House of Commons—His
death—The Duke of Chandos' bowling green at Stanmore
—Petitions for a warrant (Privy Seal) on final accounts
relating to the army—Lord Henry Brydges assumes
the courtesy title of Marquis of Carnarvon—The Duke
of Chandos erects a residence and other buildings at Bath
—S. Humphreys' poem, entitled "Canons," dedicated
to his Grace—The Duke's tenants in Middle Scotland
Yard petition the Treasury—His Grace's projected residence in Cavendish Square—Marriage of Henry, Marquis
of Carnarvon—A servant of the Duke's waylaid—Sale of
the Advowson of Rotherhithe—The Duke and Barnet
Races—Another of his servants waylaid and robbed—The
poet Young inscribes his poem, "Imperium Pelagi," to the
Duke—Alexander Pope describes Canons in his poem
called "Moral Essays"—Public feeling upon the attack.

In 1726, John, Marquis of Carnarvon, entered
the House of Commons as M.P. for Steyning,
Sussex, in place of Major-General Pepper. Unfortunately, he did not live sufficiently long to
permit of any opinion being formed of his probable success as a legislator ; he died April 5th,
1727, much to the regret of his family and
friends, from an attack of small pox.

The time-honoured game of bowls, appears to

have been considered too plebeian a pastime to
be indulged in at Canons, whose princely owner,
however, unwilling to deprive his guests of such
an old English game, had a piece of ground on
which a handsome pavilion was erected, laid out
at Stanmore for the purpose. It is said that his
Grace built a Dower house at Stanmore for his
Duchess.

Many would consider fourteen years sufficient
time to complete the audit and inspection of
the accounts concerning his Grace's late position
as Paymaster-General; but, by a petition[1] dated
May, 1727, he evidently considered from that the
accounts were being too expeditiously audited !
The Duke asserted that sundry of these, amounting to 14,612*l*. 9*s*. 6*d*., were only just complete ;
and prayed that a warrant (Privy Seal) might
issue for this amount on his final account. As
this document is unendorsed, I am unable to
present the reader with the views of their Lordships of the Treasury on the subject.

Lord Henry Brydges was relieved, in July, 1727,
of any apprehension as to his succession to the
courtesy title of Marquis of Carnarvon, and as
heir apparent to the Dukedom of Chandos. His
late brother's wife gave birth to a daughter,

---

[1] Redington's Calendar of Treasury Papers.

much, no doubt, to the disappointment of that lady and her relatives. Pending this event, his lordship appears to have been called by the courtesy title, and is so described when taking part in the coronation of George II.

The Duke of Chandos, in 1727, appears to have recovered in some measure his pecuniary position ; he rebuilt at Bath, for a residence, a house that formerly belonged to Lord Robert Brook, and also built a court of houses containing five residences, all from the designs of Mr. Wood, a local architect of repute. His Grace likewise obtained some property contiguous to the Hospital of St. John the Baptist (an old charitable institution of Bath), but he could not rebuild his property without disturbing the occupants of that institution. The Duke therefore arranged with the trustees, that the whole should be demolished, his Grace undertaking to rebuild the hospital in return for some favours shown regarding the building line of his property ; this arrangement, it is said, gave the occupants of the hospital more room and comfort.

The Duke was again honoured, in 1728, with poetic effusions. These were upon his estate of " Canons," by S. Humphreys, a poet whose fame has not been handed down to posterity. The

composition is of a similar character to that by
Gildon, some years before, therefore the reader
shall not be troubled with any of . this tyro's
warblings. Why they were ever produced or
published is a matter of amazement, unless it
were to find a patron in the Duke; but this
motive does not appear to have been successful.

The subjoined extract from a petition [1] presented to the Lords of Treasury during December, 1728, is curious, as showing the difference
in procedure for the redress of grievances in
those days from the method of our time.
Messrs. P. Farewell and R. Moore, wharfingers
of Middle Scotland Yard, Whitehall, state that
they are under-tenants of a piece of ground,
situate in that yard, adjoining the River Thames,
which was granted to the Duke of Chandos
and his heirs, with free liberty of making a
wharf for the loading and carriage of goods.
In October last, the wharf was broken up to
make a drain, whereby petitioners have been
prevented from doing any work, by which they
have not only lost their business, but also
their customers, and must be ruined unless relieved. Minuted, " It is a common sewer, and
the inconvenience, if any, must be submitted

[1] Redington's Calendar of Treasury Papers.

to." This petition is interesting from another
point, showing that Father Thames, at that
time, was sufficiently deep to permit of barges
being discharged on what has been *terra firma*
since the building of the Thames Embank-
ment.

The changes that had occurred in the Duke's
fortune prevented him from carrying out his
original intention in respect to building a new residence in Cavendish Square. It is also difficult
to fix the exact date of the erection of the two
brick mansions that are [1] still to be seen there,
one at the corner of Harley Street, the other
at the corner of Chandos Street; [2] both houses
form the termination of the north side of
Cavendish Square. Many writers have assumed
that the houses were intended as wings to the
proposed edifice. This is extremely doubtful:
on reference to the plan showing the elevation
proposed, I am inclined to believe that they were
built as separate residences to make the ground
remunerative; one of them being used as the
residence of his Grace, until he should be able to
cover the intervening space with a more magnificent edifice. The space was kept boarded or
walled in for many years, in fact until after the

---

[1] In 1892.   [2] Chandos House.

Duke's death, when the residences now standing upon it were erected.

On December 21st, 1728, Henry, Marquis of Carnarvon, was married to the daughter of Lord Bruce, with great ceremony. On the Sunday following, the Queen Consort and several lords and ladies of her Court, were pleased to wear the favours presented to them on the occasion of the marriage, when they attended divine service at the Chapel Royal.

One of his Grace's servants was waylaid and robbed on the road to Canons in the January of the next year, the thieves relieving him of one guinea and a half, though he fortunately saved three guineas by dropping them into his boots. Owing to the dangerous condition of the road it is a matter of surprise that these attacks were not more frequently made upon the Duke and his retainers.

In 1730, his Grace sold, to the Master and Fellows of Clare Hall, Cambridge, the advowson of Rotherhithe, which he had acquired in 1721. The exact reason for the sale of the patronage cannot be traced.

During September of the same year, Barnet Races were held. This may be information to readers interested in sporting matters, though the meeting is now numbered amongst the bygones; in fact, few probably know that it ever flourished. The following will show the way in which the Duke of Chandos interested himself at this meeting, the " Tuesday began the horse races at Barnet, when Mr. Jones's mare, Sweetest when Naked, was distanced the first heat by a stone horse, unknown, who won the plate, by which very considerable sums of money were lost by the jockeys, who laid great odds. On Wednesday, the 5*l.* plate was won by Townsend's galloway, and a buck, given by the Duke of Chandos, was won by Mr. Nash's horse." The buck, no doubt, was the product of his Grace's park at Canons.

Upon the evening of the last mentioned day, another of the Duke's domestics was attacked by two highwaymen in going from London to Canons. The robbers came up to him a little beyond Kilburn turnpike, and made him dismount, whereon they led him into an adjacent field, the better to search him without molestation, though their captive had nothing on him worthy the name of booty. To revenge themselves in a measure, and also to prevent their captive from raising an alarm, they bound him with his garters, leaving him in the field, where he lay until between

M

eleven and twelve o'clock the same night, before
he could attract the attention of a passer-by.

Young, the well-known author of "Night
Thoughts" and other poems, produced, in 1730,
his *Imperium Pelagi*, a novel lyric, written in
imitation of Pindar's manner. The lyric was
written to commemorate his Majesty's return from
Hanover in the September of the former year,
together with the succeeding Peace. This work
he inscribed to the Duke of Chandos, whom he
refers to in the Prologue or Argument, thus :—

> " Plenty's a means, and joy's the end,
>   Exalted mind their joys extend,
>   A *Chandos* shines, when other joys are done,
>   As lofty turrets, by their height,
>   Retain the rays of the declining Sun,"

and again, towards the close, the following
occurs :—

> " Nor *Chandos !* thou the Muse despise
>   That would to glowing *Actœon* rise,
>   (Search Pindar's breast) thou Theron of our time.
>   Seldom to man the Gods impart
>   A Pindar's head, a Theron's heart
>   In life, or sing how rare, the tune sublime."

In the following year, Pope, the immortal bard
of Twickenham, wrote his poem of " The Use of
Riches," dedicated to his patron, the Earl of
Burlington. This production was one of the

series entitled "Moral Essays," and in it he alludes to the Duke of Chandos, under the name of Timon (not a happy comparison). The references made will interest the reader, who, by this time, probably knows more concerning the 'Princely' Chandos than the 'note of interrogation' ever knew.

> " At *Timon's* villa let us pass a day,
> Where all cry out: 'What sums are thrown away!'
> So proud, so grand: of that stupendous air,
> Soft and agreeable come never there.
> Greatness with *Timon* dwells in such a drought
> As brings all Brobdignag before your thought.
> To compass this, his building is a town,
> His pond an ocean, his *parterre* a down:
> Who but must laugh the master, when he sees,
> A puny insect, shivering in the breeze !
> Lo ! what huge heaps of littleness around,
> The whole a laboured quarry above ground.
> Two Cupids squirt before a lake behind:
> Improves the keenness of the northern wind.
> His gardens next your admiration call,
> On every side you look, behold the wall !
> No pleasing intricacies intervene,
> No artful wildness to perplex the scene:
> Grove nods at grove, each alley has a brother,
> And half the platform just reflects the other.
> The suffering eye, inverted nature sees,
> Trees cut like statues, statues thick as trees,
> With here a fountain, never to be played ;
> And there a summer-house, that knows no shade :
> Here *Amphitrite* sails through myrtle bowers ;
> There gladiators fight, or die in flowers ;
> Unwatered all the drooping sea horse mourn,

M 2

And swallows roost in Nilus' dusty urn.
My lord advances with majestic mien,
Smit with the mighty pleasures to be seen :
But soft—by regular approach—not yet,
First through the length of yon hot terrace sweat ;
And when up ten steep slopes you've dragged your thighs,
Just at his study-door he'll bless your eyes.
His study ! with what authors is it stored ?
In books, not authors, curious is my Lord ;
To all their dated backs he turns you round ;
These *Aldus* printed, those *Du Sueil* has bound,
Lo ! some are vellum, and the rest as good
For all his lordship knows, but they are wood.
For *Locke* or *Milton* 'tis in vain to look,
These shelves admit not any modern book.
And now the chapel's silver bell you hear,
That summons you to all the pride of prayer :
Light quirks of music, broken and uneven,
Make the soul dance upon a jig to Heaven,
On painted ceilings you devoutly stare,
Where sprawl the saints of *Verrio* [1] or *Laguerre*,
On gilded clouds in fair expansion lie,
And bring all Paradise before your eye.
To rest, the soft cushion, and soft dean invite,
Who never mentions *hell* to ears polite.
But hark ! the chiming clocks to dinner call ;
A hundred footsteps scrape the marble hall,
The rich buffet well coloured serpents grace,
And gaping Tritons spew to wash your face.

---

[1] Pope is quite right to place this name supposititiously, though a little research would have prevented his perpetuating a mistake, still retained by many. Verrio died in 1707, some years before Canons was begun, and therefore, after the rebuilding of St. Lawrence's, Whitchurch, some of whose decorations are attributed to this artist (Verrio).

[2] Laguerre, however, was a pupil or disciple of Verrio's.

Is this a dinner? This a genial room?
No, 'tis a temple, and a hecatomb.
A solemn sacrifice, performed in state,
You drink to measure, and to minutes eat,
So quick retires each flying course you'd swear
Sancho's dread doctor and his wand were there.
Between each act the trembling salvers ring,
From soup to sweet wine, and God bless the king.
In plenty starving, tantalized in state,
And complaisaently helped to all I hate.
Treated, caressed, and tired, I take my leave,
Sick of his civil pride from morn till eve;
I curse such lavish cost and little skill,
And swear no day was ever passed so ill.
Yet hence the poor are clothed, the hungry fed;
Health to himself, and to his infants bread,
The labourer bears: what his hard heart denies,
His charitable vanity supplies.
Another age shall see the golden ear
Imbrown the slope, and nod on the *parterre*,
Deep harvest bury all his pride has planned,
And laughing *Ceres* reassume the land."

These lines confirm what has already been
stated respecting the grandeur of Canons, though
the poet, with others, takes exception to some
want of taste, which lavish expenditure does not
always atone for. In making comparison between
his Grace and Timon, Pope evidently had in his
mind the old fable of the ' ass and the dying
lion,' inclining probably to the belief that as his
Grace's fortunes were upon the wane, he would
be able to point the finger of scorn at him with

impunity. The poet's judgment was evidently at fault, as the populace testified by their dissent from the attack on one for whom they entertained much respect. This revulsion caused Pope to prevaricate in a manner unworthy of his reputation. In fact, it is difficult to find a 'parallel case in Pope's career in which the public so thoroughly disagreed with the poet's muse.

CHAPTER XVII.

Pope denies that the Duke of Chandos was meant for the
'Timon' of his poem—Letters upon the subject in the
Daily Courant—Pope personally addresses the Duke on
the matter—His Grace's reply—Lady Betty Germain
alludes to this controversy in a letter to Dean Swift—Bill
passed for vesting certain lands appertaining to the Dukedom of Chandos—Hogarth caricatures Pope—The Duke of
Chandos lends his house at Bath to the Prince of Orange.

THE reader of these pages has seen enough to
justify the popular presumption that the lines of
Pope clearly point to Canons and the Duke of
Chandos. The poet soon found he had raised a
hornet's nest about his ears, in the form of
dissent from his views, though at every opportunity he strenuously denied the application.
Such proceedings made matters worse than an
open apology would have done, the denial giving
greater publicity to the attack. Thereon Pope
found he had overstepped the bounds of prudence,
though he still persistently disavowed the application, not only in public, but also in his private
correspondence; an instance of this is shown in
the following letter to Aaron Hill.

"Twickenham, December 22nd, 1731.

"DEAR SIR,—I thank you for your Tragedy,
which I have now read over a sixth time, and of
which I not only preserve, but increase my
esteem. You have been kind to this age in not
telling the next in your preface, the ill taste of
the town—of which reception you describe it
to have given of your play, more, indeed, than I
had heard, or could have imagined—is a more
flagrant instance than any of those trifles
mentioned in my epistle, which yet I hear the sore
vanity of our pretenders to Taste flinches at extremely the little you mention had been a
properer[1] to that epistle, I have heard no
criticisms about it, nor do I listen after 'em. "*Nos
hæc minimus esse nihil.*" I mean I know the
verses to be so, but as you are a man of tender
sentiments of honour, I know it will grieve you
to hear another indirectly charged with a crime
his heart is free from, for if there be truth in the
world, I declare to you I never imagined the
least application of what I said of Timon could be
made to the Duke of Chandos, than whom there
is scarce a more blameless, worthy and generous
beneficent character among all our nobility, and
if I have not lost my senses, the town has lost

[1] I give the letter in its original form.—J. R. R.

'em. By what I heard so late as but two days
ago of the uproar upon this head, I am certain, if
you calmly read every particular of that description, you'll find almost all of 'em point blank the
reverse of that person's villa, it's an awkward
thing for a man to point in defence of his own
work against chimera, you know not who or what
you fight against, the objections stand up in a
new shape, like the armies and phantoms of a
magician, and no weapon can cut a mist or a
shadow. Yet it would have been a word in justification against a most malicious falsehood—I
speak of such as have known by their own
experience these twenty years, that I always took
up their defence, when any streams of calumny
ran upon 'em—if it gives the Duke one moment's
uneasiness, I shall think myself ill-paid, if the
whole world admired the poetry, and believe me
would rather never have written a verse in my
life, than any one of them should front, to a truly
good man. It was once my case before—but
happily reconciled—and among generous minds
nothing so endears friends, as the having offended
one another. I lament the malice of the age,
that studies to see its own listeners in everything : I lament the dulness of it that cannot see
an excellence. The first is my unhappiness, the

second yours; I look upon the fate of your
piece, like that of a great treasure, which is
buried as soon as brought to light, but it is sure
to be dug up the next age.

" I have been very sensible in these two
occasions to feel them—as I have done—at a time
when I daily fear'd the loss of—what is and ought
to be dearer to me than my reputation, but that
of a friend, or anything except my morals—of a
most tender parent, she is alive and that is all.
I have perceived my heart in this, and you may
believe me sincerely,

" Dear sir,

" Your faithful and affectionate servant,

" A. Pope."

The foregoing letter has an important bearing
on the controversy, and one that appears to have
escaped research by many in alluding to this
matter; but the denial did not and will not stand
the test of comparison with the references so
pointedly made.   The letter appears to be almost a plea *ad misericordiam* on the writer's
behalf, and to intimate that Mr. Hill should
enter the arena of public opinion in defence of
the poet.   Again, Pope somewhat overacts his
disavowal by dwelling upon the popularity and

public character of the Duke of Chandos. This serves to make the epistolary satire still more calumnious; nor does Mr. Hill appear to have thrown himself into the 'breach' in his friend's defence.

On the next day, the following letter appeared in the *Daily Courant*, December 23rd, 1731:—

" To John Gay, Esq.[1]

" Sir,—Had the author—of the Epistle on Taste—attacked vice, at a time when it is not only tolerated, but triumphant, and proclaimed with ostentation, as a merit, I should have been under some apprehension for the consequence.

" 'Tis said the satire is personal. I thought it could not be so, because all its reflections are on things, and not on persons, not on the man, but on his house and gardens, pictures, statues, trimmed trees, and violins.

" Some fancy that to say a thing is personal is the same as to say it is unjust, not considering that nothing can be just but what is personal. I am afraid, such writings as teach no man, will mend no man.

" The application of Timon's character to the Duke of Chandos, is monstrous as it imputed, to

[1] The poet Pope's friend, patronized by the Duke of Chandos.

the person the most different in the world from a man hater, and whose taste and encouragement of wit have ever been shown in the rightest place. This author has always been distinguished and favored by this very person, besides, is his garden crowded with walls? Are his trees cut into figures of men? Do his basons want water? I am sick of such foolish applications."

The letter does not bear any signature, assumed or otherwise. Why it is addressed to the poet's compeer Gay is uncertain, unless he had remarked the want of " taste " in his friend Pope's application. The other communication that appeared conjointly with the above, runs as follows :—

"To A—— P——E, Esq.

" SIR,—You insinuate as if vice was authorized by law, and so triumphant, as not to be opposed without ill consequences, at a time when the laws against immorality were never so strictly executed since the Reformation. Are not the following personal?

> " Who but must laugh, the master when he sees
> A puny insect, shivering at a breeze !
> Behold, my Lord, advances o'er the green,
> Smit, with the mighty pleasures to be seen."

" By the word just, you must mean like, and by unjust injurious, for the more just—like—a personal reflection is, so much the more unjust—injurious—it must be, so that these insinuating men seem to reason very like.

"If you had consulted your Scotch retailer of Boyle, and Moren, he would tell you that Timon was first eminent for his extraordinary generosity, the abuse of which drove him into a hatred of mankind! viz.,

> "Treated, caressed, and tired, I take my leave,
> Sick of his civil pride, from morn to eve."

"It is a known trick amongst lampooners, when a man is to be ridiculed to draw the remarkable lines of his picture, beyond the life, yet with such resemblance, that all the world may cry ''Tis he.'"

Like the letter preceding, this one also bears no signature, and both are fair specimens of the letters which appeared in the controversy. Some asserted that it was unworthy of the poet to assail a man of rank and generosity, who was popularly credited with having befriended Pope by a gift of 1000*l.*; but here again, common report was a common perverter of the 'truth,' as Pope himself denied this, nor does there appear to be any foundation for the rumour. Pope still endeavoured to allay the public irritation by all kinds of subterfuges, going so far as to indite an apology under the *nom de plume* of *Cleland*. But the artifice was no more successful than his dissimulation. He was driven at last to indite an exculpatory letter to the Duke himself. His Grace answered with magnanimity, as a man accepting the excuse without believing the professions, remarking "that to have ridiculed his taste or his building, had been an indifferent action in another man, but from him, after the reciprocal kindness that had been exchanged between them, it was less easily excused." This is one rendering of part of the reply forwarded by the Duke; another runs thus, " he took the application that had been made, as a sign of malice of the town, against himself, and seemed very well satisfied it was not meant for him." As no verbatim copy of this correspondence can be traced, the reader must accept the references mentioned, though which is correct it is difficult to say, but either shows the spirit in which the reply was couched.

Lady Betty Germain, the correspondent of the famous Dean Swift, alludes to Pope's discomfiture in a letter to the Dean, dated

"January 11th, 1731-2.

.   .   .   .

"I met with your friend Mr. Pope the other

WILLIAM HOGARTH'S PLATE 'TASTE.'

Page 175.

day; he complains of not being well, and indeed looked ill. I fear th at neither his wit or sense do arm him enough against being hurt by malice, and that he is too sensible of what fools say, the run is much against him on the Duke of Chandos's account, but I believe their rage is not kindness to the Duke, but glad to give it vent, with some tolerable pretence of truth. . ."

Pope found himself next year attacked by Hogarth, who is alleged to have been patronized by the Duke of Chandos. In the well-known plate called "The Man of Taste," by that eminent painter and engraver, Pope is represented as whitewashing the gate of Burlington House, bespattering the coach of his Grace of Chandos as it passes. The force of this caricature is as keen to-day as when it appeared, satirizing the poet's patron, as much as the poet had satirized by his pen the Duke of Chandos. This probably led Pope the next year to attempt a peace-offering to the public and his Grace, by mentioning the latter in a poem termed the "Characters of Men," in these words,—

"Thus gracious Chandos is *beloved* at sight,"

a somewhat fulsome eulogy after his previous allusions in the Epistle on Taste,—

"Sick of his civil pride from morn to eve," etc.

Hogarth's production, however, appears to have established a truce between the poet's muse and those whom it had offended; though, by the irony of fate, Pope's prophecy that—

"Another age shall see the golden ear
 Imbrown the slope, and nod in the parterre,"

became true, metaphorically speaking, by the dismantling and piecemeal sale of the costly fabric and its surroundings.

Leave was given this year—1731—by the Upper House, to bring in a Bill vesting certain manors and hereditaments in the said Duke and his heirs, pursuant to certain articles of agreement made upon the marriage of his son Henry Brydges, commonly known as the Marquis of Carnarvon, with the Honourable Mary Bruce, eldest daughter of Charles, Lord Bruce. The Bill passed the Lords and was thereupon sent down to the Commons, who approved it without any amendment, and shortly after it received the Royal Assent. The bearer of the message of concurrence with the Bill, from the Lower House, was the then well-known 'Long' Sir Thomas Robinson.

In January, 1734, the residence of the Duke at Bath was accepted by his Serene Highness

the Prince of Orange, for a sojourn there while
taking the waters. Upon arriving, the Prince
dispatched an express to his Grace, at his house
in St. James's Square, intimating his safe arrival
with but little fatigue. Bath still retains a record
of this visit of his Serene Highness.

CHAPTER XVIII.

Dean Swift and the Duke of Chandos—The Dean's verses on
his Grace—Lady Betty Germain and the Dean—Mrs.
Pendarves and the Dean—The Duke of Chandos' letters in
· the Egerton MSS. collection—Death of his Grace's chaplain and of the second Duchess of Chandos.

ANOTHER literary giant of those days has handed
the Duke down to posterity in prose and verse,
to wit, the celebrated Dean Swift, of St. Patrick's,
who addressed his Grace under date of August
31st, 1734, thus :—

" MY LORD,—Although I have long had the
honour to be an humble servant to your Grace,
yet I do not remember to have ever written you
a letter, at least, since her Majesty's death, for
this reason, your Grace will considerably wonder
to find a man wholly forgotten, begin or commence by making a request, for which I can offer
no other excuse than that frequent application
has been made to me by many learned and
worthy persons of this city and kingdom, who
having heard that I was not unknown to you,
seldom failed any opportunity of pressing me to

solicit your Grace—of whose generous nature
fame has well informed them—to make a present
of those ancient records on paper or parchment,
which relate to this kingdom—Ireland—which
were formerly collected, as we have heard, by
the late Earl of Clarendon, during his government here, and are now [1] in your Grace's possession. They can be of no use in England, and
the sight of them will be of little value to foreign
virtuosos, and they naturally belong to this poor
kingdom. I could wish they were of great
intrinsic value, so as to be sold on the Exchange
for a 1000*l.*, because you would then part with
them at the first hint, merely to gratify your
darling passion of generosity and munificence,
and yet since they are only valuable in the place
of their birth, like the rest of our natives, I
hope you will be prevailed on to part with them
at the humble request of many very deserving
persons in this City and University, in return for
which bounty the memory of it shall be preserved
in that honourable manner which so generous a
patron of learning, as your Grace, will be cer-

---

[1] The MSS. referred to was a collection made by Sir James
Ware, the celebrated Irish antiquary, during the seventeenth
century, afterwards acquired by Lord Clarendon, son of the
historian, during 1686, and purchased on his death by the
Duke.

tainly pleased with, and at their request alone, I desire your compliance, without the least mention of myself as any way instrumental.

" I entreat your Grace's pardon for this interruption, and remain, with the greatest respect,

" My Lord,
 " Your Grace's, etc., etc.,
  " Jon. Swift."

Certainly this was a bold request by one not easily abashed, though why his Grace should part with the MSS., simply because he was requested to do so by the Dean (admittedly on behalf of other persons) seems strange, especially so when it was known the Duke had acquired them by purchase, showing a desire to possess them. Had he, on the other hand, acquired these documents by bequest or inheritance, the demand would not appear so singular. The Dean, however, wisely cloaks his demand by an ardent appeal to his Grace's generosity. Nevertheless, the demand was not complied with ; the denial being accepted as a personal rebuke by the Dean, who has immortalized the request by these verses :—

" James Brydges and the Dean had long been friends,
James is be-duked, and so their friendship ends ;
And sure, the Dean deserves a sharp rebuke,
From knowing James, to boast he knows a Duke,

"Yet since just Heaven the Duke's ambition mocks,
Since all he got by fraud is lost by stocks,
His wings are clipped, he tries no more in vain,
With bands of fiddlers to extend his train.

"Since he no more can build, and plant, and revel,
The Duke and Dean seem more near a level.
O wert thou not a Duke—my good Duke Humphrey
From bailiffs' claws thou scarce could'st keep thy — — free,

"A Duke to know a Dean ? Go, smooth thy crown,
Thy brother,[1] far thy better, wore a gown.
Well, but a Duke thou art, so pleased the King,
Oh! would his Majesty but add a string."

These lines evince irritation, no doubt, heightened by his Grace denying any acquaintance with him (the Dean). The latter, determined not to desert his quest, called in the aid of other persons to accomplish that which he could not effect alone, and addressed himself with this object to Lady Betty Germain, who replies to the Dean under date of November 7th, 1734 :—

"I have no acquaintance with the Duke of Chandos, nor, I believe, has the Duke of Dorset, much, and to be sure, it would be of no purpose to ask him for those records again, because if he would have parted with them, he would have done it at your asking."

Nothing daunted, the Dean approached another lady correspondent of his, viz., Mrs. Pendarves, who replied as follows :—

[1] The Rev. Henry Brydges, D.D.

"St. Mary's Square,
"Gloucester,
"November 20th, 1734.

.   .   .   .   .

"As soon as I received your letter, I went to
your brother Lansdowne, and spoke to him about
the Duke of Chandos ; he desired me to make his
compliments, and to tell you he was very sorry
he could be of no service to you in that affair,
for he has had no manner of correspondence, or
even acquaintance, with the Duke these fifteen
years. I have put it, however, into other hands,
that will pursue it diligently, and I hope, obtain
for you what you desire; if they do not succeed,
you must not call me negligent, for whatever lies
in my power to serve you is of too much consequence for me to neglect. . . ."

But this lady's efforts on the Dean's behalf
were as futile as others.

His Grace's favour at Court still continuing, he
received during December, 1734, a grant from
his Majesty King George II., for working all the
royal mines of gold and silver that were already
or may be, discovered in the county of Stafford,
and to work, melt, smelt, and refine the same.
Had this grant been for the more plebeian, but
useful metal, iron, or even coal, his Grace's

descendants (who were expressed in the patent) would have found themselves possessed of almost untold wealth. Whether the Duke attempted to make use of his grant I have not been able to discover. This patent may surprise even some of our present day mineralogists.

Amongst the Egerton MSS. is a portion of a letter (appended) in the handwriting of the Duke of Chandos, though to whom addressed I cannot trace, but, by the footnote, presumably to a relative of Lord or Lady Dysart."

"January 4th, 1735-6.

"Of honour speak it, from association, but from real fear, that you have by your character of $M^{r.}$ (minister) raised [1] her expectations so high, that when I come to wait on her, she may find the original—for she hath never seen me—fall so short of ye picture, as to create a disgust that may not be wiped off.

"I am, dear Sir,
"With utmost truth,
"Your most obliged and humble servant,
"CHANDOS."

[Note appended.]

[1] If this letter were dated a year later, another construction might be placed on it.

"I can't but take notice of one thing; that in all this transaction, I don't find L. D. (Lady Dysart) hath ever hinted her brother should be made acquainted with it, this motive would imagine she perhaps thinks it not so proper to be communicated to him; to be sure the more ye power is looked into, the more better it is."

This note hardly seems to coincide with the matter expressed in the text, as that refers to some person who had never seen his Grace, and this could scarcely have been the case with Lady Dysart, his late son's mother-in-law.

The Rev. Hugh Shorthouse, chaplain to the Duke of Chandos, and lecturer at Chelsea, died early in February, 1735. This reverend gentleman was without doubt the Duke's town chaplain, as it has already been shown that the Rev. Dr. Desaguliers held a similar appointment at Canons.

On the 14th Feburary, his Grace again addresses his, to us unknown, correspondent. This communication relates to the matter mentioned in the note appended to the first-mentioned letter, and runs thus :—

"February 14th, 1735-6.

"DEAR SIR,—I have received much to my surprise a letter just now from Lady D., something more kind than her last, she writes me word, she'll consider of this affair and give me a positive answer on ye 6th of March. I go out of town this morning, and will stay at Shawhall, till ye 2nd of March, when I propose God willing to return to Cannons (Canons) in order to be in town, at Essex Buildings on ye day she hath appointed, to receive her final answer, she cannot keep me I think in suspense, if she doth not intend to comply at last, it will be a most serious, and unheard of usage, if she would. I return you all imaginable thanks for your friendship, and desire you to be assured I will on all occasions,

" With ye utmost readiness
" Approve myself
" Dear Sir,
" Your most obliged, faithful servant,
" Chandos."

By this it appears that his Grace was seeking some favour (possibly of a pecuniary nature), from her ladyship; and one which was evidently of importance, as the word 'serious' occurs in the text. This letter was answered, notifying fresh developments in the matter, as is shown by his Grace's reply dated

" Shawhall,

" February, 21st, 1735-6.

" DEAR SIR,—I return you many thanks for
your obliging letter which last post brought me,
and for ye trouble you have given yourself in
speaking again to Mr. C., concerning ye affair in
hand, shortly after what hath past, and this
fresh time that is taken to consider of it, one can
hardly imagine, but that ye lady's reputation
will be such, as I could wish, should it prove
otherwise, I shall have great reason, to think
ye usage I have met with to have been very
hard. I must desire you will make my compliments to Mr. C. and take an opportunity of
seeing him again, in this interval, to know how
matters are like to go, for I don't expect to hear
myself anything further of it, till I return in
order to which I propose setting out for
Cannons (Canons) on Monday, or Tuesday
furnight—fortnight—as I think there is a good
deal of likelihood that this matter will end as I
desire, I must beg you will be very cautious in
what you hint, with regard to anything that you
may have in view, and since ye success cannot
fail to be determined in a few days it will
certainly be better not to make your boast of it

whatever in anything till ye fate of this is
seen.

"I return ye draught (draft) you sent me for
ye next presentation to spare, it is a Rectory,
but it will be proper, it should be filled up with
your son's name, because I have been asked for
it for a nephew of my own, who is in orders,
and I gave for a reason why I could not do it,
because I had already promised it your son.

"I am with great truth
"Your most faithful humble servant,
"CHANDOS."

Whatever this mysterious business may have
been it was not ultimately concluded, as the
following shows :—

"March 10th, 1735-6.

"DEAR SIR,—Since I saw you I have some
reason to desire you will not take any steps in
ye affair you mentioned, when I tell you why I
desire it, you will be astonished, I believe at it,
and more when ye faithlessness is assured you.
I don't, however, think ye other will come to
anything, so great is ye unsteadiness of some
people, but this I am very sure of, that your

friendship lays me under such obligations to you that you shall ever find me,

"Dear Sir,

"Your most faithful and obliged servant,

"CHANDOS."

Reference having been made to the possible cause of this correspondence, it only remains to be said that his Grace's financial resources were evidently much strained at this period.

On July the 19th, 1735, the second Duchess of Chandos died of an apoplectic fit which seized her while on a visit to the Honourable Mrs. Brydges at Avington, Haywood's Hill, Middlesex. This seizure occurred on a Monday afternoon, and she lingered, though speechless, until the following Wednesday, when she expired. The Duchess is said to have been a model of exemplary piety and conjugal affection, combined with a sweet and benevolent disposition, and was one whose loss was severely felt by all who knew her.

CHAPTER XIX.

His Grace assists the Colonists for the new State of Georgia—
Monument to the Prince of Orange at Bath—The Duke
of Chandos mentioned as likely to receive the vacant
Garter—Letter from his Grace to the Duke of Newcastle
—Marriage of the Duke of Chandos to Lady Davall—The
controversy concerning this lady fully discussed, and her
identity substantiated—His Grace of Chandos made
captain of the Yeoman of the Guard—The strained relations between King George II. and the Prince of Wales—
His Majesty's opinion of Henry, Marquis of Carnarvon
—Letter of condolence from the Duke of Chandos to Sir
Robert Walpole—The Duke and Duchess of Chandos
present at the private interment of Queen Caroline, consort
of George II.

THE Duke of Montagu having given a quantity
of workmen's tools, such as were used by car-
penters, joiners, smiths, etc., to the settlers
proceeding to the new State of Georgia, the
Duke of Chandos and several of the nobility
and gentry also became generous benefactors to
the new Colony.

The townspeople of Bath availed themselves
of the visit of the Prince of Orange to Bath,

previously alluded to, to name one of the squares
of that town after his Highness. In further com-
memoration a pillar was erected in the centre of
the square, bearing a Latin inscription which,
translated, reads thus :—

"The Prince of Orange was happily restored
to health by drinking the waters of Bath,
through the favour of God, and to the extreme
joy of Great Britain, 1735."

The reader need not be reminded, that the
Prince of Orange espoused the Princess Royal,
daughter of George II.

The retailers of gossip were busy this year
as usual, circulating the rumour that the Duke
of Chandos was to have the Garter, vacant
by the death of the Earl of Peterboro. This
premature unofficial bestowal of the sovereign's
favour was again wrong, for though his Grace
received many other orders and favours, he never
attained to that dignity.

About this period, 1736, it appears, by the
following communication addressed to the Duke
of Newcastle, that some persons had been either
trespassing on, or damaging, his Grace's property in Herefordshire; the exact particulars
are wanting. The following letter, however,
throws a little light on the matter :—

"February 12th, 1736-7.

"My Lord,—Pursuant to your Grace's commands I write by this post to the Trustees of the turnpike in Herefordshire, for the original information they took concerning the cutting down that walk (which) was got up at Wilton, and to acquaint me. With the goodness of his Majesty, through your Grace's instruction is pleased to show to me, by your issuing a proclamation offering a reward for the bringing to justice, any of the offenders; and so soon as I receive the original information I will have the honour to lay them before your Grace.

"I am with ye greatest truth and respect,

"My Lord,
"Your Grace's
"Most obedient and
"Most humble Servant,
"Chandos."

9 months!

On April 14th, 1736, the Duke of Chandos entered the holy bonds of matrimony for a third time. The lady was not his equal in social rank, being the widow of Sir Thomas Davall, Kt., M.P. for Harwich, an opulent London merchant. Lady Davall brought the Duke 40,000l., a small

sum in comparison with the formerly large
fortune of his Grace. The marriage was not
made for mercenary motives, though probably
the bride's fortune was acceptable to the Duke
in his then straitened circumstances. The
wedding ceremony, which was almost of a
private nature, took place at the residence of
Lady Davall in Conduit Street, W.; the happy
pair proceeding in the evening to his Grace's
domain of Canons.

The truth concerning this marriage has been
distorted, and, in many instances, erroneous
accounts have been given of it. In fact, this is
only one of many instances where the biographer
or memoir writer has not hesitated to accept the
dicta or *scripta* of one who may have heard or
known a little of a circumstance, without being
acquainted with the whole of the facts. In this
way errors are perpetuated for generations, to
the discredit of aspirants for literary fame. In
the foregoing case the error was originated by
one of Dean Swift's numerous correspondents, a
Mrs. Pendarves, who, in an epistle to the Dean,
under date of April 22nd, 1736, states :—

·   ·   ·   ·   ·   ·

"The Duke of Chandos's marriage has made

a great noise, and the poor Duchess is often
reproached with (her) being bred up in Burr
Street, Wapping."

. . . . . .

Now the facts, so far as I have been able to
discover, do not show that, Lady Davall was
either bred or born in Burr Street, Wapping—
(Lower East Smithfield)—as at this period the
Vanhattons, Vannottens, or Vanhattens (the
name is spelt in various ways), of which family
she was a member, were merchants of high
repute residing in Devonshire Square, Bishopsgate, then considered a highly respectable place
of residence for opulent city merchants. The
family of Burr or Burre likewise followed mer-
cantile pursuits, principally with Holland, and
were brother merchants, long established in the
parish of St. Botolph, Bishopsgate, at Barking
and elsewhere in Essex. It was upon a portion
of this family's estate that Burr Street was
built. The Davalls became connected with the
Burrs by the marriage of the first Sir
Thomas Davall, Kt., and M.P. for Harwich,
with Rebecca, daughter and heiress of Daniel
Burr or Burre of Amsterdam and London.
This lady was the mother of a numerous

o

progeny, the eldest of whom received the honour
of knighthood, and succeeded his father in the
representation of Harwich, Essex, in which
county he owned a good estate, principally
through his mother, as heiress of the Burrs.
This Sir Thomas's sister, Lydia, married John
Vanhatten, thus connecting the three families
of Burr, Davall, and Vanhatten. The above-
named Sir Thomas, who married Lydia
Catherine Vanhatten—John Vanhatten's sister
—bequeathed by his will the greater portion of
his estates in Essex, which he had inherited
through his mother, to his cousin, David Burr;
in fact, he gave back to this family their former
possessions, leaving no issue of his own to
inherit. Thus there is really little or no proof of
the aspersions cast by Mrs. Pendarves on the
bringing up of this lady; but they might have
gone down to posterity unnoticed, except for
the fact that every scrap of writing relating to
the Dean of St. Patrick's has been collected
and published, thumbed, and read for generations past, and quoted as fact by compilers
until now : thus far for the first assertion.
The second is far more ludicrous and also more
erroneous than the first, and has been perpetuated by greater would-be authorities. This

is no less than the assertion that the third and
last wife of the Duke of Chandos (Lady Davall),
had been the wife of a brutal ostler, from whose
violence the Duke was supposed to have
rescued her at the George Inn, Glastonbury,
or the Castle or Pelican's hostel at Newbury
or Winchester ; the authorities themselves not
being certain as to the locality. The Duke
is then said to have sent her to school
(having purchased her, or satisfied her
husband for her loss) to remedy defects in
her education, and to have married her
later. It is most extraordinary how this
romance concerning the third wife of the
first Duke of Chandos has been handed down
and believed. It has also served as plot for
a writer of fiction, being worked into a novel by
Miss Spence, in a work entitled, " How to be
Rid of a Wife," now a scarce book, though
published only in the thirties of this century.
This narrative, in which the noble 'hero' is
termed Belmore, seems to have taken possession
of the reflective faculties of a very estimable
old gentleman named Clark (*circa* 1836), who
published a book at this period entitled " Reminiscences of Handel," in which he alludes to
this matter as an absolute fact, though it was

unsupported by any trustworthy evidence, and
goes so far as to assert that the lady was a Mrs.
Carter. This is only further addition to the
misconception, as the whole matter in no way
concerns the first Duke of Chandos, or the lady
who became his third wife. To Henry, the
second Duke, son of the first holder of that
dignity, must be assigned this strangely chival-
rous proceeding—as such it is (at least, for the
latter end of the so-termed " Augustan " age in
England). Henry, when Marquis of Carnarvon,
lost his first wife in 1738, and married his second
on Christmas Day, 1744, four months after he had
succeeded to the dukedom. This person was the
reputed ostler's wife or widow, Anne Wells or
Jefferyes by name. Her family were in poor
circumstances, as is testified by a gentleman of
that period named Thicknesse, who states that
upon arriving at Southampton from a visit to
Jersey in 1752, he took lodgings opposite the
market-place, and was daily accosted by a good-
looking young woman who kept a stall there
for the sale of greengrocery. Her naïve manner
of saying, " Nothing in your way to-day, sir? "
attracted Mr. Thicknesse's attention. Afterwards he was informed by a friend that this
marketwoman was one of the then Duchess of

Chandos' sisters. The next morning he asked for further information from her Grace's sister, who substantiated the report, adding to her interrogator's question, as to whether "her sister the Duchess took proper notice of her," "That she did, and though she had many sisters, her sister sent for them all up to London, when she would give them new clothes suitable to their station, send a servant to show them the sights of the town, besides make them a present of money, and pay their coach fare back to the country," concluding with "What else could she do? for we are not fit to sit down to the Duke's table." Mr. Thicknesse further asserts that the Duchess had been a pot-girl to an ale-house at Winchester, although, beyond the fact that she was of lowly origin, and her name Anne Wells or Jefferyes, there is no corroborative testimony that can be relied on to support the purchase from an ostler, or the wife theory. The Duchess died July 8th, 1757, and is stated to be buried in Keynsham Churchyard, Somerset. In an almost 'up to date' work,[1] the compiler follows and cites Mr. R. Clark's erroneous assertions concerning the third wife of the first Duke of Chandos. On the other hand,

[1] Cassell's Greater London.

the whole tenour of the article relating to the
Duke bears evidence of a visit to Whitchurch,
where the tomb in the monument room of the
Brydges family, in the Whitchurch Parish Church,
sets forth faithfully who the first Duke's third
wife was, but appears to have been overlooked.

Though Society of that period no doubt
looked down upon the Duchess because she
was connected with 'trade,' the first Duke
of Chandos found in her a good wife and
a congenial companion, as his own testimony
proves.

In the following year, 1737, his Grace received
additional proofs of Royal favour, being appointed
Captain of the Yeomen of the Guard, in the
room of the Earl of Ashburnham, deceased; his
son Henry, Marquis of Carnarvon, was, however,
in anything but good grace with his Majesty
George II. at this time, as the following
testifies.[1] Lord Hervey conversing with his
Majesty George II. upon the strained relations
between that monarch and the Prince of Wales,
his Majesty replied to some comments made by
Lord Hervey, saying: "That those about him,
(the Prince of Wales) must see and feel this dis-

[1] Hervey Memoirs.

tinction, and cannot fail, though he should not find
it out, to represent it to him. Who about him,"
urged the King, " will tell it him? or who about
him indeed has sense enough to find out anything?
Who is there, but boobies, and fools, and roadmen
he ever listens to?" Lord Hervey laughed, and the
King went on : " Why, is it not so? There is my
Lord Carnarvon,[1] a hot-headed, passionate half-
witted coxcomb, with no more sense than his
master. . . ."

This exhibition of warmth against his Grace of
Chandos's son, did not prevent the King from
showing friendship and favour to the Duke.
The King's estimate of " my Lord Carnarvon " may probably explain that peer's later
marriage with Anne Wells ; it certainly shows
him in a light that others have failed to throw
upon him.

Lady Walpole, wife of the famous Sir Robert,
the great minister during the reign of the first
two Georges, died August 20th, 1737. Therefore,
as one in corresponding Court favour, the Duke
of Chandos pens the annexed letter of condolence to
his friend, the bereaved husband. The letter bears
date some months after the sad event; but news

---

[1] Henry, Marquis of Carnarvon, a Lord of the Prince's bed-
chamber.

travelled slowly then, although this in itself does not account for the lapse. Probably his Grace was visiting at some distance from London when the event occurred; the delay, however, does not detract from the sympathy expressed.

"Canons, November 12th, 1737.[1]

"Sir,—I have just received the terrible news the town is so much alarmed with. The sincere respect and affection I have for you, fill me with such grief, that though I cannot be silent, I know not how to express myself. I condole with you from the bottom of my heart, on the very great and severe loss you are about to receive. I beg of God that His providence will continue, still in its full vigour, to those noble spirits and abilities, which have for such a number of years so wonderfully supported you, under the many heavy trials you have had. That this misfortune, great as it is to everyone, may be attended with no personal ill, is the most ardent prayer of

"&c. &c.
"Chandos."

During the following month of December, his Grace had another melancholy duty to perform;

[1] Cox's Memoirs of Sir Robert Walpole, 1798.

no less than to be one of the attendants (with his
Duchess) upon the chief mourners at the private
interment of Queen Caroline, Consort of his
Majesty George II., which took place the night
of the 17th December, in the Collegiate Church,
Westminster.

CHAPTER XX.

Death of the Marchioness of Carnarvon—The Duke of Chandos
elected a Governor of the Foundling Hospital—His Grace's
correspondence with the Duke of Newcastle at this
period—Death of the Duke of Chandos, August 9th, 1744
—Memorial lines—Inscription on his monument—His son
Henry, Marquis of Carnarvon, takes his seat as 2nd Duke—
Petitions for leave to bring in a Bill to sell part of the
estate—Leave granted—Nature of the Bill, etc.—Library
at Canons sold, *circa* 1745—Sale of pictures in London,
removed from Canons—Catalogue of same—Remarks.

THE first wife of Henry, Marquis of Carnarvon,
died at Twickenham, August 19th, 1738, after a
long illness, leaving two children, a son and
daughter, who, with many friends, public and
private, mourned her loss. His second marriage
was the romantic adventure alluded to in the
preceding chapter, by which Anne Wells or
Jeffreyes became Duchess of Chandos.

The Duke of Chandos, during 1739, was
elected one of the Governors of the Foundling
Hospital : evidently another tribute to the Duke's
reputed business abilities, for the welfare of others,
as they had not been altogether successful in his

own affairs. Except when discharging the duties connected with his office and Court appointments, the Duke now led an almost retired life; that he sometimes interested himself by aiding friends seeking appointment or promotion is shown in the following letter, addressed to the Duke of Newcastle :—

"October 12th, 1741.[1]

"My Lord,—His Majesty having been pleased, I understand, to give Colonel Murray leave to sell his commission, and leave it for ye Lords' Regents to sign such other commissions as shall be necessary thereupon, and your Lordship having fixed upon Major Halden of ye 4th troop of Horse Guards to succeed him, I make it my humble request to yr Grace, that if you are not otherwise engaged, you will have ye goodness to notice with your powerful interest, ye pretensions of Captain Peters, Brigadier and Lieutenant in ye 3rd troop of Horse Guards, to succeed ye aforesaid Major Halden. This young gentleman is a neighbour of mine in ye country, hath been several years in the service in Lord Albemarle's troop, and hath gained ye esteem of all who knew him. Your Grace taking notice of him on

[1] Newcastle MSS.

this occasion, will lay a great obligation on him, who, with greatest respect,

> " My Lord,
> " &c. &c.
> " Chandos."

The Duke of Newcastle had long been acquainted with his brother peer; therefore no doubt the request was granted, as is confirmed by another favour demanded later.

The letter runs as follows, corroborating at the same time, that the Duke of Chandos resided in Cavendish Square, as the communication is addressed from—

> " Cavendish Square,[1]
> " November 4th, 1743.

" My Lord,—Having heard that a new Commission of ye Peace is going to be made out for ye County of Middlesex, I humbly take ye liberty of putting your Grace in mind of the two gentlemen I recommended to you, viz. Mr. John Asgill Bucknall of Oxney, and Mr. Roger Smack of Watford, there is likewise another whom I trust ye will permit me to ask ye good favour for, a gentleman whose character is well known to ye

---

[1] Newcastle MSS.

Lord Chancellor, and who will be a very careful
person in discharging the duty of that office, is
in my neighbourhood, it is Mr. Francis Capper,
Councillor-at-Law, of Lincoln's Inn.

> "I am, with great respect,
> "&c.   &c.
> "CHANDOS."

This triple request savours of 'Oliver asking
for more,' but no doubt the Duke knew how far
he might trespass on his Grace of Newcastle's
good nature.

On the 9th of August, 1744, the Duke of
Chandos paid that debt of Nature's which all
mortals sooner or later must, dying at his seat
of Canons, after an illness of three weeks.

Thus passed away one who played no mean
part in the affairs of his country. Some may
object to this assertion with respect to his post
of Paymaster-General, held during the most
brilliant part of Marlborough's career. But it
will be scarcely necessary to remind the reader
that no specific charge of fraud was made
against his Grace; while the way in which the
populace championed him proves that he was no
ordinary man, being able to endear himself for a
lifetime to such a fickle jade as Public Opinion,

for many would have been anathematized and disgraced, on a charge not a thousandth part so grave as that connected with the Pay Office. On the other hand, it must be admitted that much of the esteem he won was by his natural magnanimity and tact. This would lead one to imagine that the system then prevalent of conducting the public finances and offices was in fault, and not the man, as it is hard to suppose that a person credited with the good qualities his Grace was, could be guilty of striking out a 'crooked' path for himself. Should such a surmise be correct, then it is only just to admit that he followed in the footsteps of his predecessors, while the wars that raged during his tenure of office largely increased the funds passing through his hands, much to the benefit of " Self and Co."

The above is submitted with all due deference. The reader, however, will form his own opinion, being placed in possession of the most important facts—many published for the first time—relating to the Pay Office.

The following lines upon the death of the Duke were published in the *Gentleman's Magazine*, 1744 :—

"And he is gone, the gentlest noble mind,
The Lover and the Love of human kind,
Chandos, whose wealth by every virtue graced,
Showed how Heaven's bounty shines when justly placed.
So true a judge, and patron to desert,
A hand so generous, and so pure a heart,
That innocence thro' sorrow smiling beamed,
And *want*, with graceful eyes, his praise proclaimed.
All who could feel his warmth, his power confessed,
And all who felt it owned such greatness blessed,
Nor let the Muse, who feels his absence most,
Deplore his virtues or example lost.
A Brydges, formed by Heaven, is left behind,
Heir to his worth, his titles, and his mind,
Whose gentle ear, like his to me, shall bend,
Whom Science grateful shall revere her friend ;
This checks our anguish, for such Virtues gone,
Since all the Father's merit marks the Son."

Though this effusion to his Grace's memory does not bear the stamp of the poet laureate of that period, it nevertheless shows the esteem in which the late Duke had been held. The last lines are open to doubt, or at least require corroboration.

The remains of the Duke were interred in the Brydges family vault, in the Parish Church of St. Lawrence, Whitchurch, or Little Stanmore. Over his body was erected a handsome marble monument, with a life-size figure of his Grace in a Roman dress, standing between his first and second wives. Underneath is an inscription, of which the following is a translation :—

" In hope of a joyful resurrection, here lieth the body of the most noble James Brydges, Duke of Chandos, Marquis and Earl of Carnarvon, · Viscount Wilton, Baron Chandos of Sudeley, and a Baronet, member of his Majesty's most Honourable Privy Council, Lord-Lieutenant and Custos Rostolorum of the County of Radnor, a High Steward of Cantremelewith, Chancellor of the University of St. Andrew's in Scotland, Ranger of Enfield Chace, one of the Governors of the Charter House, who was born January 6th, 1673, and departed this life August 9th, 1744. Whose modesty ordered all encomiums on his tomb to be avoided, yet justice to his memory and truth tell the reader that, if a youth spent in constant application to business, which tended more to the good of his country, and friends, than his own, a whole life passed in acts of greatest humanity, and charity, forgiving every one, and giving to the utmost of his power, ended an old age, dedicated to patience, resignation, and piety, deserve from mankind gratitude and love, they are most strictly his due.

" He married first, Mary, daughter of Sir Thomas Lake, of Canons, in Middlesex, by

whom he left the Most Noble Henry, Duke of
Chandos; his second wife was Cassandra,
daughter of Sir Francis Willoughby of Wollaton,
and sister to Thomas, Lord Willoughby; his third
wife was Lydia Catharine, daughter of John
Vanhatten, Esq., and widow of Sir Thomas
Davall, Kt., who was a Member of Parliament,
and died in the year 1714."

Referring to a remark made in the preceding
chapter, the following extract from his will
will testify to the late Duke's opinion of his
third wife : " I owe the greatest comfort I have
enjoyed in this life—since I have been blessed
with her—to my Duchess Lydia Catharine."
He further expresses a wish that on her death
she shall be buried in the vault with himself,
also that her figure in marble shall be placed
upon his monument at a cost of not more than
200*l.* This clause, owing to some disagreement
with the second Duke, was not carried out in its
entirety. Lydia, dowager-Duchess of Chandos,
directed by her will that she should be interred
at Stowe, but her remains were exhumed afterwards, and placed beside her husband the Duke
at Whitchurch. The provision respecting the
statue was, however, not fulfilled.

According to the law of primogeniture, Henry,

P

Marquis of Carnarvon, the eldest surviving son
(five others having predeceased him) succeeded
to the Dukedom of Chandos. The Marquis at
this period was M.P. for Bishop's Castle, Shropshire; he was also Groom of the Stole to H.R.H.
the Prince of Wales. He took his seat in the
House of Lords as second Duke, November 27th,
1744.

That the estate left by the late Duke was much
encumbered, is proved by a Petition presented to
the House of Lords by Henry, second Duke of
Chandos, and Anne his wife, 1745,[1] on behalf of
themselves, and Charles, Earl of Aylesbury—a
trustee—for and on behalf of James Brydges
(eventually third and last Duke of Chandos in
direct descent), commonly called Marquis of
Carnarvon, and Caroline Brydges, his sister,
commonly called Lady Caroline Brydges, both
infants, the only issue of the said Duke by Mary,
his late wife, lately called Marchioness of Carnarvon, one of the daughters of the said Earl
(Aylesbury). The Petition prays leave to bring
in a Bill for sale of a sufficient part of the estates
settled by deed of lease and release of the 31st
of May, 1734, made in pursuance of the agree-
ments entered upon, previous to the marriage of

[1] House of Lords Journals.

the said Duke, then styled Marquis of Carnarvon, to raise money to pay off certain mortgages, named in this petition, and for several other purposes.

The Petition was ordered to be referred to the Lord Chief Justice of the Common Pleas, and Mr. Baron Clarke, with the usual directions, according to the standing orders, duly reported on it. Leave was then given to bring in a Bill for the purposes asked, intituled ' An Act for vesting part of the settled estates of the Most Noble Henry, Duke of Chandos, in trustees for raising money to discharge encumbrances, etc.' The Bill, after having been discussed by a committee appointed by the House of Lords, was approved, and then sent down to the Lower House for confirmation.

Here is proof beyond cavil of the decadence of the 'Grand' Duke's fortune. During his latter days especially he managed to keep up appearances, and to reside at Canons until the last, but at the cost of encumbering the estate. The Bill above alluded to contained a clause for the sale of the mansion-house and effects at Canons. The first part sold was the library, during 1745. But little is known of the distribution of the late Duke's valuable collection of books and MSS.

It was not until 1747 that the mansion and effects were dispersed; it took nearly two years to prepare these for the auctioneer's hammer. The edifice itself was thought too large and costly for any possible tenant; it was therefore pulled down, and the materials were sold in lots.

The pictures were removed to London for sale, and, as a catalogue has been preserved, I am able to give an account of them, together with some comments upon them by that celebrated and discerning connoisseur George Vertue.

" A catalogue of the genuine collection of pictures of his Grace James, Duke of Chandos, lately deceased, consisting of a variety of valuable paintings (pictures) by the most celebrated Italian, French, and Flemish masters, which must be sold by auction, by Mr. Cock, at his house in the Great Piazza, Covent Garden, on Wednesday, May 6th, 1747, and the two following days.

" The said collection may be viewed at the place of sale, on Saturday, the 2nd of May, and every day after, Sunday excepted, till the time of sale, which will begin each day, at half an hour after eleven, catalogues of which may be had gratis, at Mr. Cock's aforesaid. Conditions of sale as usual.

THE DUKE OF CHANDOS' TOWN HOUSE IN CAVENDISH SQUARE.　Page 213

" N.B.—In the last day will be sold (by order of the trustees, at the special desire of the creditors) his late Grace's dwelling house in Cavendish Square,[1] with all the land thereunto belonging, and an equal moiety of the reservoir,[2] now let to the York Buildings Company, at 150*l.* per annum, payable to his Grace, agreeably to the printed conditions of sale, delivered gratis.

" And in each day's sale will be sold four lots of marble statues (life-size), some time since brought from Naples.

" FIRST DAY'S SALE.

" WEDNESDAY, MAY 6TH, 1747.

1. Italian.   The Decollation of St. John.
2. Holbein.   Sir George Blage, three-quarters.
3. Raphael (after).   A Madonna in a round.
4.   „   A woman's head, large as life.
5. Italian.   A piper's head.
6. „   A martyrdom.
7. „   A landscape.
8. „   Its companion.
9. Verelst.   A piece of flowers.
10. Pelegrini.   Mars and Venus.

---

[1] This must have been bought in or other arrangements arrived at, for ever since the first Duke's death it remained in the possession of the family or their descendants until it was pulled down early in 1892. The house in the extreme right-hand corner of plate was the Duke of Chandos', and a *replica* of the house at the other corner.

[2] This is the reservoir mentioned in connection with the York Buildings Waterworks.

11. Titian (after). A dead Christ.
12.   „   A hermit with a death's head.
13. Cornelius Janssen. King Charles I.
14. Hendekooter. A piece of birds.
15. Perugino. A Madonna.
16. Poelenburgh. A small landscape and figures.
17. Marco Ricci. A neat landscape and figures, in water colours.
18. Marco Ricci. A sea triumph, on glass.
19.   „   Apollo with figure, dancing, in *chiarascuro.*
20. Guido. Jacob stealing the blessing from his brother Esau.
21. Guido. Its companion, Hagar and Ishmael.
22. Borgione. A battle.
23.   „   Its companion.
24. Weenix. A boy fleaing a dog.
25. Italian. A Madonna with St. Francis.
26.   „   Vandyke's head, with a sunflower.
27.   „   A man's head, with a scroll of paper.
28.   „   Its companion.
29. Raphael (after). The Virgin, our Saviour, and St. John.
30. Pietrida Cartona. The marriage of St. Catherine.
31. Weenix. A dead hare and birds.
32.   „   A basket with flowers of curious needlework.
33. Raphael (after). The Transfiguration.
34.   „   Heroditus with the head of St. John.
35. Paul Weenix. A Saint, with an angel and cross.
36.   „   St. Francis, its companion.
37. Guercino. A boy bit by a lizard.
38. Gascar. A nobleman, half-length.
39.   „   Its companion.
40. Mr. Wooton. A long landscape and figures.
41.   „   A winter piece—its companion.
42. Titian. A man's head, with a pen in his ear.
43. Holbein. Ditto, with a book.
44. Romanelli. Danæ and the golden shower.

45. Wyck. A battle, three-quarters.
46. Titian. Susannah and the Elders.
47. Sir Peter Lely. Mrs. Franklin, half-length.
.48. Palamedes. A consecration.
49.   „   Its companion.
50. Schidone. The Virgin, our Saviour, St. Elizabeth and St. John.
51. Rottenhamer. The feast of the Gods.
52. David Teniers. A Dutch kitchen.
.53. James Bassano. Jacob's journey into Egypt.
54.   „   Its companion, Noah sacrificing after coming out of the Ark.
55. Guido. The flight into Egypt.
56.   „   Its companion.
57. Miens. A young gentleman, a small half-length.
58. Gerard Dow. A Market.
59. Asland. Jupiter and Leda, in *chiara-scuro*.
60. Sir P. P. Rubens. The offering of the three kings.

"SECOND DAY'S SALE.

" MAY 7TH, 1747.

61. Holbein (after). A man's head, three-quarters.
62.   „   Oliver Cromwell.
63. Spagnoletto. Lucretia.
64. Italian. A landscape and figures.
65. Buckhuysen. A sea piece.
66. Titian (after). A lady, half-length, with a lap-dog.
67. Holbein. Charles Brandon, Duke of Suffolk.
68. Giorgione. A general, half-length.
69. Zeeman. Boys drawing by candle-light.
70. Franciscus Floris. A feast of the Gods.
71. Vandyck (the style of). A large family picture.
72. Father Seegero. A Holy Family, with a festoon of flowers.
73. Italian. Hercules and Omphâle.

74. Italian. A Madonna.
75. „ A landscape in water colours.
76. „ A Holy Family, in water colours.
77. „ A Dead Christ.
78. Vande Velde. A small sea piece.
79. Douk v. Ryswich. A parrot in a festoon of flowers of mother-of-pearl, curiously inlaid.
80. Paul Veronese (after). The marriage of St. Katherine.
81. Laresse. A Bacchanalian.
82. Holbein. A man's head in a round.
83. „ A siege ; a drawing heightened with gold in a brass frame.
84. Italian. A long landscape, with figures.
85. Rembrandt. David and Nathan.
86. Buckhuysen. A sea piece.
87. Luca Judano. The Virgin in the clouds.
88. Holbein (after). A small half-length of Oliver Cromwell.
89. Italian. A Madonna with other figures.
90. Paul Veronese. The Adoration of the Kings.
91. „ Its companion.
92. Bredal. Two small landscapes with figures and houses.
93. Rottenhamer. The Nativity.
94. Rubens. Constantine, etc.
95. Paul Veronese (the style of). The marriage of St. Katherine.
96. Nicolas Poussin. Perseus with the head of Medusa.
97. Rubens. Ceres with a cornucopia, and a Satyr with a flute.
98. Rubens. A bas-relievo of Louis XIV. and sixty-three Intaglios of the ancient Kings of France.
99. Rubens. A man playing on a guitar.
100. A nun and a friar.
101. Guercino. St. John.
102. Titian (after). An Ecce Homo.
103. Vandyck. A Holy Family.
104. Jordans of Antwerp. A family picture.
105. John de Bellini. A Holy Family.

106. Vandyck. A man's head, with a roll of paper in his hand.
107. Cornelius Janssen. Its companion.
108. Gerard Dow. Boys at school.
109. Vanderneo. A Magdalen.
110. Dobson. Mr. Killigrew, half-length.
111.   „   King James I., a whole length on horseback.
112. Sir Peter Lely. Lady Dean, and Mrs. Franklin playing a guitar.
113. Sir G. Kneller. Mr. Knight, the famous singer and favourite of King Charles II., half-length.
114. Titian. A Holy Family, with St. Jerome.
115. Giorgione. A musical conversation.
116. Guido. A Madonna.
117. Salvator Rosa. St. George and the dragon.
118. Seb. Boudin. The finding of Moses.
119. N. Poussin. Hercules preferring Virtue to Vice.
120. Sir P. P. Rubens. Charles the Fifth of Spain, big as life, on horseback, with Fame holding an olive wreath.

"THIRD DAY'S SALE.

"MAY 8TH, 1747.

121. Two drawings in Indian ink, and a Chinese lady's head.
122. A Madonna in water colours.
123. Our Saviour and the Samaritan woman in water colours.
124. A limning of the Assumption of the Virgin.
125. A curious bas-relievo, in ivory, of Jupiter and Leda.
126. Poelenburgh. A Magdalen, with angels
127. Cornelius Janssen. A lady, half-length.
128. Titian. A Holy Family.
129. Giorgione (school of). The martyrdom of St. Peter.
130. Wyck. A landscape with figures and horses.
131.   „   Its companion.
132. Carlo Dala. Our Saviour's head, an oval.

133. Carlo Dala. Its companion.
134. Cornelius Janssen.—Hervey, Esq., three-quarters.
135. Romanelli. Lot and his daughters.
136. Lucca Jordan (after). A Venus.
137. Verelst. Two pictures of the seasons.
138. P. Anullo. A large piece of still life.
139. Italian. St. John.
140. Titian. A cardinal, half-length.
141. Sir G. Kneller. The Duke of Marlborough.[1]
142. Vandyck. A charity.
143. V. Vande Velde. A sea fight.
144. Wyck. A large battle.
145. „ An old man's head, three-quarters.
146. „ Its companion.
147. Vandyck (after). King Charles the First, in three attitudes.
148. Vandyck. A Madonna with angels, in a landscape.
149. N. Poussin (after). A sacrifice to Bacchus.
150. Laroon. A conversation, in an oval.
151. Paris Bourdon. A Madonna and a St. John.
152. Poelenburgh. Cimon and Iphigenia.
153. Walker. King Charles I. (painted when a prisoner at Hampton Court) and the Prince of Wales.
154. Seb. Ricci.[2] The Salutation of the Virgin, a design for one of the chapel windows at Canons, and the worshipping of the golden calf, its companion.
155. Seb. Ricci. Two ditto of the Nativity and the Ascension of our Saviour.
156. Seb. Ricci. Two ditto, the stoning of Stephen, and our Saviour with two disciples at Emmaus.

---

[1] Though the Duke of Marlborough does not appear to have been on friendly terms with his brother peer, he entertained sufficient respect for the great General to have his portrait at whole length by the first delineator of that day.

[2] Sebastiani Ricci. Italian artist, 1670—1734.

157. Seb. Ricci.   Two ditto of St. John baptizing our Saviour, and the healing of the lamb.
158. Seb. Ricci.   Two ditto, the Virgin and St. Elizabeth, and the Adoration of the Kings.
159. Seb. Ricci.   Two ditto of our Saviour walking on the sea, and the conversion of St. Paul.
160. Eight cartoons, after Raphael.
161. M. Angelo de Battaglia.   A conversation.
162. Paul Veronese.   Our Saviour's Passion in the garden.
163. N. Poussin.   A Bacchanalian.
164. Holbein.   Erasmus, a small three-quarters.
165. Rottenhamer.   Silenus with nymphs.
166. David Teniers.   A gallery.
167. Titian.   A Dead Christ.
168. Taddeo Zaccaro.   The entombing of our Saviour.
169.   „   Nine miniatures of King Charles II., etc.
170. Gerard Dow.   A gentleman playing the violin.
171.   „   A lady playing the virginal.
172.   „   Its companion, a woman with a basket of fruit.
173. Sir P. Lely.   The Duke and Duchess of York, half-length.
174. Rubens.   A sleeping Venus, a Hermit, and the Devil.
175. Pordinone.   The Virgin, our Saviour, and St. John.
176. Rubens.   The tribute money.

" N.B.—Cavendish House, and the lands thereunto belonging, to be sold in six lots agreeably to the printed conditions of sale.

" FINIS."

The above constituted a small but select collection of pictures by old and modern masters. If those without names attached and the copies are omitted, the number is considerably reduced, though the quality remains. Had the examples of Holbein, Titian, Rubens, Paul Veronese, Salvator Rosa, Gerard Dow, David Teniers, Guido, Sir Peter Lely, and Sir Geoffrey Kneller, alone been retained by the second Duke, his descendants would have been able to dispose of them, at the present day, for far more than their weight in gold. What some were then sold, or rather sacrificed for, will be seen in the next chapter.

CHAPTER XXI.

George Vertue's notes on some of the pictures sold from Canons
—Sale of the mansion in lots, and other effects—Ultimate
destination of some of the most noteworthy parts of the
chapel and edifice—Sale of the advowson of St. Lawrence,
Whitchurch, and of the Manor of Totteridge—The Duke,
as Groom of the Stole to H.R.H. the Prince of Wales,
receives commands from H.R.H. respecting the wearing
of French stuffs by his Court—The statue of King George I.
from Canons re-erected and uncovered, November 19th,
1748—The second Duke of Chandos known to have re-
sembled his father in one particular at least—Finis.

GEORGE VERTUE, engraver, connoisseur, and art
critic, attended the sale of the late Duke of
Chandos' pictures, and with the minuteness of
detail that characterized him, has left a MS.
account of his visit, together with the prices
fetched by several of the most noteworthy pictures. These in some instances were low enough
to make many collectors of to-day wish they
had lived in the times of long ago, if only to
have benefited their descendants, when such
works of art could be purchased at prices that
embryo academicians of to-day would consider
too paltry for even their immature efforts.

Vertue acknowledges that in the Duke's collection
were many curious pictures, and thought lot 47,
by Sir Peter Lely, a very fine specimen of that
master. Lely's picture sold for the magnificent
sum of 12l. 10s.; whilst lot 52, a specimen of
that great Dutch master David Teniers, depicting
" a Woman asleep in a kitchen," and pronounced
by this authority " a complete picture," changed
hands at 35½ guineas. Lot 59, a long drawing
in chiaro-scuro by Asland, he mentions "as worthy
of record;" lot 97, a fine piece of clear trans-
parent colouring, representing " Ceres with a
cornucopia, and a Satyr with a flute," by the
great Peter Paul Rubens, was knocked down for
45 guineas; lot 108, " Boys at School," by Gerard
Dow, sold for 42l. 10s. 6d. Eight sketches in
oil for the chapel windows at Canons, by Seb.
Ricci, fetched 48 guineas (gold frames included);
lot 160, eight cartoons in water colours, after
those of Raphael at Hampton Court, by Goupy,
sold for 17l. 6s. (the Duke paid Goupy 300
guineas for them); lot 170, a fine specimen of
Gerard Dow, dated 1636, was bought for 88½
guineas; its companion, lot 171, " A Lady playing
on the Virginals," found a purchaser at 50l. 10s.;
another specimen of this master's art, lot 172,
changed hands at 64 guineas; lot 173, by Sir

Peter Lely, " The Duke and Duchess of York,"
fetched only 14*l*. 10*s*.

The foregoing will give an idea of the artistic
value of the collection as a whole, and may tend
to enlighten art lovers as to the value of the
old masters at that period.   It also informs us in
whose possession these works have been, and
confirms their authenticity.

A month or so following the dispersion of the
pictures, the contents of the mansion at Canons
were sold ; and so numerous were the lots that
it became the rage, for the moment, for persons to
possess something as having once belonged to
the ' Grand ' Duke or ' Princely ' Chandos ; therefore few who attended came away empty.   The
finale arrived at last, and Canons, as a ducal
residence, ceased to exist, being razed to the
ground and the materials sold in lots.   The
greater part of the materials were bought
with the estate by Mr. William Hallett, a
wealthy upholsterer of Long Acre, London,
who purchased the several lots at such a low
price, as to enable him, after erecting a fair-
sized residence upon a portion of the old
site, to acquire almost a small fortune by the
judicious re-sale of material not required for
his own purposes.   The two porters' lodges

he allowed to remain, having them transformed, by skilful additions and alterations, into handsome villas, which were afterwards inhabited by Colonel Lindsay and F. Aitken, Esq. The whole of the building materials brought the trustees only 11,000*l.*, or about five per cent. of their original cost, a shrinkage never anticipated by the noble founder of Canons, but fully corroborating the old saying, "Fools build and wise men buy;" although this implies that if there were no fools there would be no buyers.

The most important and handsome parts of this unfortunate residence found other resting places. The great portico and pillars were purchased by Earl Tylney, for his magnificent but unfortunate mansion, erected afterwards at Wanstead.[1]

The marble staircase and pillars of the grand entrance hall were sold to the Earl of Chesterfield, who used them to beautify his house in Mayfair, and where they still are. The witty Stanhope was wont to term these his 'canonical' pillars.

Among the numerous and costly articles of *vertu* was a piece of carving, by the famous

[1] There are many prints of this mansion still extant.

PRESENT HOUSE AT CANONS.

Page 224.

Grinling Gibbons, representing the Stoning of Stephen; the architectural parts of the design were particularly well executed. This carving had remained for many years at the carver's house at Deptford, where he followed the pursuit of ship carving, until it was unearthed by John Evelyn, who furthered Gibbons' interests by recommending him to the notice of King Charles II., who appointed him his wood carver. This post he held during the four succeeding reigns. The piece of carving from Canons was purchased by the owner of Bush Hill Park, Enfield, whose hall it adorned for many years.

The handsome altar, pulpit, font and pews (arranged like choir stalls when in the private chapel at Canons, demolished with the rest of the building) and attributed to Grinling Gibbons, though more probably done under his supervision, were purchased by — Freeman, Esq., of Fawley Court, Bucks, and set up in Fawley Church. There they remained intact until recently.[1]

[1] The respected rector of this parish, the Rev. W. Afric Tanner, M.A., courteously informs me that some six years ago many of the oak seats were found to be so much worm-eaten and affected with dry rot, that the church was reseated, though as much of the old material was used as possible. He confirms my already expressed opinion that the carving appears to be by different hands; a document in the parish chest verifies the statement that this wood-work came from Canons.

Q

The organ,[1] by the Jordans, is said to have gone to the Church of St. John's, Southover, (Lewes). This is incorrect, as it was purchased for Trinity Church, Gosport, where it remains, and is substantiated by a note to be found in Hopkins' work on the Organ. The Chandos coat of arms on the top of the instrument also confirms it. Further proof exists in the form of a printed document, dated 1748, in possession of Mr. Howlett, at one time the church organist, showing a kind of Dr. and Cr. account concerning its acquirements, etc., which runs thus :—

	£	s.	d.
To cash paid Mr. Cock (the auctioneer) for the organ as it stood at Canons . . .	117	12	0
To Mr. Jordan for taking it down, and carriage to London	16	0	0
To Mr. Jordan for repairs	105	0	0
To do. for new swell	30	0	0
To do. for repairs and carriage to Gosport	8	0	0

The above, with other curious items, make the total cost 344l. 15s. 6d.

The stained glass window is stated by the learned Dr. Hughson (author of a " History of Middlesex "), to have been purchased by the parish of Great Malvern. Present day confirma-

---

[1] Out of the private chapel.

tion of this is wanting, as no record of such a
purchase has been found by Mr. Notts, the
compiler of an exhaustive work on the historical
and interesting Parish Church of Great Malvern,
The writer admits, however, that during the
eighteenth century this church was neglected to
the greatest degree, and much of the magnificent
stained glass ruthlessly smashed by mischievous
schoolboys, also that one window at this period
was sold to eke out a churchwarden's account !
But, even now, for all its vicissitudes, the edifice
contains some of the finest old stained glass in
the country.

The magnificent wrought iron railings, that at
one time closed the southern entrance to Canons,
now part the gardens of New College, Oxford,
though, strange to say, the learned and courteous
head of the college, Dr. Sewell, informs me
that no record of their acquirement can be
found amongst the archives of that institution ;
but he admits that tradition confirms their
purchase from Canons. Probably the 'powers
that were' in those days at the head of
"New" desired some memento of one who
had received his education at its hands, therefore they embellished their grounds with a piece
of the art of Tubal, said to have been the

work of a celebrated hammersmith of that time.
A specimen of the handicraft of the latter may
still be seen without journeying to Oxford, in the
gate to the monument room of the Brydges
family at St. Lawrence, Whitchurch. Some
railings, of less beauty and design, though
singularly graceful, were bought by the parish
of St. John, Hampstead. These consist of gates
(one[1] still closes the main entrance to the
church) and part of the railings that enclose the
church. By the favour of the Rev. Sherrard
Burnaby, M.A., vicar of the parish, I am able
to corroborate the foregoing statement by the
church records. " That at a meeting of the
trustees of the parish church, 15th June, 1747, Mr.
Sanderson, surveyor, stated that there was a
quantity of iron gates and pallisadoes (palisades)
to be sold at a public auction, at Canons, the
seat of the (late) Duke of Chandos, etc. ' Agreed '
That Mr. Vincent and Mr. Marl be desired to go to
Canons, with Mr. Sanderson, and view the above-
said, etc., and if approved, bid for and purchase
such part, as they think proper for the purpose
aforesaid." " At a meeting the 19th June, 1747,
Mr. Vincent and Mr. Marl reported that they had
bought at the sale at Canons, about fifty-nine

---

[1] Said to be the private chapel gate.

RAILING IN NEW COLLEGE, OXFORD.

Page 228.

feet of iron pallisadoes (palisades) at 14s. 6d.
per cwt., the stone coping and brickwork under
it—then—included." " On the 25th July, 1747,
Mr. Vincent and Mr. Marl reported that they
have bought one other lot at the sale at Canons,
being two side iron gates, each about nine feet
wide, at 15s. 6d. per cwt."

Among the other removes were some
curiously wrought copper-gilt lamps, having
stone pediments for their bases, and used to
light the grand avenue. One of similar make,
on a much larger scale, lit the entrance hall.
Some of these were to be seen (so that well-
known antiquarian, John Timbs, affirms) at Day
and Martin's old premises in Holborn a few
years since. The author recollects an antique
lamp of singular design hanging over the
entrance there; probably this was from Canons.
No present member of the firm can affirm anything further than that some old lamps were on
the old premises at one time.

The Brydges family severed their connection
with the domain of Canons so thoroughly as to
dispose of the advowson to the Church of St.
Lawrence, Whitchurch, on which the late Duke
had spent large sums of money.

So departed the glory of Canons! Into the

history of the past went its magnificence and splendour. Fate, however, has been kinder to this spot than to many, as it has not yet been devoured by the railway demon or ruthlessly cut up for building. Though circumscribed, it is still a charming residential property, retaining almost intact the so-called "villa" erected by Hallett, since whose time the estate has changed owners repeatedly. Among the most noteworthy possessors of this historical place was Dennis O'Kelly, the owner of the famous racehorse Eclipse, who was buried in his time in its grounds, only to be unearthed and the skeleton exhibited in Mr. Bullock's Museum at the Egyptian Hall later. Sir Thomas Plumer, Master of the Rolls, was one of the next possessors of the estate. May it long continue to remain an historical property.

Whether the amount received by the disposal of the estate of Canons, etc., was insufficient for the purposes desired can only be surmised by the fact that the following year, 1748, the manor of Totteridge was sold by the Duke or his Trustees, though the adjacent manor of Kingsbury, the nearest to their late possession (Canons), was retained. The assumption is that the produce of the previous sale had failed to attain the desired ends.

It is not the purpose of this work to follow the career or fortunes of the second Duke of Chandos; they were but commonplace. However, the following may be of interest, in these days of Fair Trade demonstrations. On November 19th, 1748, the Princess of Wales' birthday, H.R.H. the Prince held a reception, and noticing several lords handsomely attired in clothes of French materials, desired his Groom of the Stole (the Duke of Chandos) to acquaint them, and all his servants, that after that day he would be much displeased to see them appear in materials of French manufacture. The same notice was also communicated to the ladies.[1]

This birthday reception took place at Leicester House (Leicester Fields), and on the occasion the statue of George I., lately brought from Canons, and re-erected in the centre of that space, was uncovered.

(Referring to the footnote on page 68 of this work, respecting a recent publication on Leicester Square, in which the date, 1748, for the re-erection of this statue, is doubted, my authority for it being correct is the November number of the *Gentleman's Magazine*, 1748.—AUTHOR.)

[1] Here is a case of 'history repeating itself,' as, in 1668, both Houses of Parliament requested King Charles to give similar commands to his courtiers.

The second Duke of Chandos did not inherit all his father's good qualities, but he imitated him in one respect—he ventured into the bonds of matrimony for a third time! True, his means were insignificant in comparison to his father's at one time, but had he possessed the same wealth, it is doubtful whether there would have been another ' Princely ' Chandos.

FINIS.

APPENDIX A.

To Mr. Brydges.[1]

Camp at Lens le Béguines.
July 13th, 1705.

Sir,—I am favoured with your letter of the 19th of June, and am very glad that upon your return, with success,[2] from your election, you found your patent ready for entering into the pay office. I assure myself of your faithful endeavours for the service of her Majesty, and advantage of the troops, will not be lost there, than they have been in other employments.

It will be much for your care to begin your accounts on a clear footing, and what you have already remitted for the Army, is a good presage of your future care of them, in which you will not want my Lord Treasurer's assistance, so you may depend on my endeavours to make your office as agreeable, as you may desire.

I am,
With truth, Sir,
Yours, &c.
Marlborough.

---

[1] Lieut.-Gen. Murray's Marlborough's Letters and Dispatches, 1845.

[2] Re-election for Hereford, upon accepting appointment.

APPENDIX B.

Camp at Terbanck,
2nd July, 1708.

To MR. BRYDGES.[1]

SIR,—I was very glad to understand by your favour of the 4th ult., that you were returned to Town,[2] with so much satisfaction and success. The provision that was made for you in another place, when you found yourself opposed at Hereford, will I hope convince you of the just sense your friends have of your inclinations, and abilities to serve her Majesty and the nation. You may be assured I shall be always ready to promote what may be agreeable to you.

I believe our long continuance in the camp has been a great disappointment to our friends at home. I assure you it has been no less so to me, after the measures I had concerted with the Elector of Hanover, and Prince Eugene in April last, but I hope we shall be able in a little time to send you some good news, for I have an account that Prince Eugene's Army has been on the march towards us these four days. The Prince himself designs to be at Maestricht the 4th, in order to come directly to the camp, and the horse three or four days after, and if they can join us before the enemy have their troops from the Saire, I think we need desire nothing more.

I am with truth,
Sir, &c.
M.

APPENDIX C.

Brussels, February 4th, 1709.

To MR. BRYDGES.[1]

SIR,—I received two days since your favour of the 2nd

------

[1] Lieut.-Gen. Murray's Marlborough's Letters and Dispatches, 1845.

[2] Speaking of his re-election for Hereford.

of January, and though I am very sensible I may depend upon your friendship, yet I am not sorry you received the opportunity of expressing it on the late occasion, in the manner you might have been inclined to do, for I am of opinion that in those matters the less said the better. I hope my services will need no apology with good men, and as long as they may be of any benefit to the public I shall be very little concerned at the endeavours any others may use to lessen them.

I am very glad my Lady Marlborough has given you such perfect satisfaction upon the late groundless discourse of removes, and shall myself readily embrace all opportunities of assuring you that I am with truth

&c. &c.

M.

APPENDIX D.

Camp before Douay,
15th May, 1710.

To MR. BRYDGES.[1]

SIR,—I have received your obliging letter of the 24th past, and return you thanks, for your kind congratulations on the successful opening of the campaigns. . .

I am very well satisfied, I may always depend on your friendship, and shall be glad on all occasions to give you first assurances of the truth.

Wherewith I am,
Sir, &c. &c.

M.

17th July, 1710.

To MR. BRYDGES.[1]

SIR,—I received yesterday the favour of your letter of the

---

[1] Lieut.-Gen. Murray's Marlborough's Letters and Dispatches, 1845.

21st of June, and am very much obliged to you for the kind part you take in our successes here, we should be very happy if they could contribute towards quieting and calming the ferment at home, which otherwise may unravel whatever it is possible for us to do on this side. I am glad Lady Marlborough prevented you in your application to succeed Mr. Howe. I assure you, no man but yourself shall have my good wishes towards it, and whenever the employment became vacant, I will readily do my part in such a manner as you shall think most effectual.

> Being with truth,
> Sir, &c. &c.
> M.

APPENDIX E.

!September 8th, 1710.

To Mr. Brydges.[1]

Sir,—I am favoured with your letter of the 18th past, and am very sensible of the concern you were in at the removal of my Lord Treasurer, you may guess by it what mine must have been, not only from the friendship and intimacy that has been so long between us, but more particularly for the sake of the public, which ought to be our chief care, therefore I cannot but approve of your resolution of continuing your employment, since I am persuaded it can never be in better hands, and while I have anything to say, I am sure you cannot doubt of my friendship.

I was glad to see by your letter to Mr. Cardonel, you had made such considerable remittances for the troops, with promise of 100,000*l.* more the week following, which I hope is come over, our regular subsistence here being of the last consequence to

---

[1] Lieut.-Gen. Murray's Marlborough's Letters and Dispatches, 1845.

the Service. I cannot help mentioning to you on this occasion the daily clamours I have from the Prussian troops for want of the payment of their last winter's quarters, and must pray, you will take immediate care, to ease me of their importunities.

I am with truth, &c., &c.,

M.

APPENDIX F.

Hague,
March 31st, 1711.

To MR. BRYDGES.[1]

SIR,—I am so much obliged to you for your letter of the 26th February, that I cannot omit my thanks for it, and in return for the fresh assurances you give me of your friendship, I pray you will believe nothing in my power shall ever be wanting, that may convince you of the sincerity of mine.

We have been very much disappointed for want of timely remittances for the forage. I have directed Mr. Cardonel[2] to write you as formerly, on this subject, to whom, therefore, I pray you will be referred.

I am, Sir,
Yours, &c., &c.,
M.

APPENDIX G.

July 22nd, 1711.

To MR. BRYDGES.[3]

SIR,—As busy as I am of a post night, I cannot omit writing

---

[1] Lieut.-Gen. Murray's Marlborough's Letters and Dispatches, 1845.

[2] His private secretary.

[3] Parkes' Life of Henry St. John, Viscount Bolingbroke.

to you upon a subject wherein I think myself particularly concerned. Mr. Blake made a very considerable provision of all
sorts of stores for the expedition commanded by Brigadier
Hill, as those preparations both for land and sea, were kept
private, and went almost singly through my hands; so it fell
to my share to contract on this occasion, by the Queen's Commands. The poor man I believe is half broke by being kept
so long out of his money, after having extended his credit to
the utmost stretch. My Lord Treasurer has promised to give
dispatch to this affair, and I am confident will do it, even to-
morrow morning, if you are so kind as to demand the money.
Mr. Blake is in danger of being arrested. I am sure I had
rather be so, than teased at the rate I have been about this
matter. I beg your assistance herein, and shall take it for as
great a favour, as if I was personally concerned in it.

I am, &c., &c.,

H. St. John.

APPENDIX H.

Camp at Lens,

July 16th, 1711.

To Mr. Brydges.[1]

Sir,—Your letter of the 9th of the last month is come safe
to hand, and gives me fresh instances of your friendship, which
I shall always depend upon, as you may that nothing shall be
wanting, as far as lies in my power to make you suitable
return. We must continue to do our duty, and so long as I
think, neither malice or envy can do us much harm, you will
oblige me in continuing to let me know what you think may
be worth my notice, and pray believe me with great sincerity,

Sir, &c., &c.,

M.

---

[1] Lieut.-Gen. Murray's Marlborough's Letters and Dispatches,
1845.

APPENDIX I.

Camp,
October 1st, 1711.

To Mr. Brydges[1] of the Ordnance.

Sir,—As I always intended the accounts of the application of the money issued at the Exchequer, for the building of Blenheim, should be audited with all the strictness possible, for the satisfaction of her Majesty and the public, though otherwise I am no ways accountable for it. I should be very much obliged to you, if you would take the trouble upon you, with the assistance of Mr. Mercaton and Mr. Mead or such other, as you shall think proper, who may begin the examination immediately. And upon my return, which I hope may be in less than two months, I will give you such powers or other assistance, as shall be thought necessary, being well assured my Lord Treasurer will fully approve of what you shall do therein.

I am with truth,
Sir, &c., &c.,
M.

---

[1] Lieut.-Gen. Murray's Marlborough's Letters and Dispatches, 1845.

INDEX.

ST. DUNSTAN'S HOUSE, FETTER LANE,
LONDON, E.C. 1892.

Select List of Books in all Departments of Literature

PUBLISHED BY

Sampson Low, Marston & Company, Ld.

ABBEY and PARSONS, *Quiet Life*, from drawings; motive by Austin Dobson, 31s. 6d.

ABBOTT, CHARLES C., *Waste Land Wanderings*, 10s. 6d.

ABERDEEN, EARL OF. See Prime Ministers.

ABNEY, CAPT., *Thebes and its Greater Temples*, 40 photos. 63s.

—— and CUNNINGHAM, *Pioneers of the Alps*, new ed. 21s.

About in the World. See Gentle Life Series.

—— *Some Fellows*, from my note-book, by "an Eton boy," 2s. 6d.; new edit. 1s.

ADAMS, CHARLES K., *Historical Literature*, 12s. 6d.

ADDISON, *Sir Roger de Coverley*, from the "Spectator," 6s.

AGASSIZ, ALEX., *Three Cruises of the "Blake,"* illust. 2 vols. 42s.

ALBERT, PRINCE. See Bayard Series.

ALCOTT, L. M. *Jo's Boys*, a sequel to "Little Men," 5s.

—— *Life, Letters and Journals*, by Ednah D. Cheney, 6s.

—— *Lulu's Library*, a story for girls, 3s. 6d.

—— *Old-fashioned Thanksgiving Day*, 3s. 6d.

—— *Proverb Stories*, 3s. 6d.

ALCOTT, L. M., *Recollections of my Childhood's Days*, 3s. 6d.

—— *Silver Pitchers*, 3s. 6d.

—— *Spinning-wheel Stories*, 5s.

—— See also Low's Standard Series and Rose Library.

ALDAM, W. H., *Flies and Fly-making*, with actual specimens on cardboard, 63s.

ALDEN, W. L. See Low's Standard Series.

ALFORD, LADY MARIAN, *Needlework as Art*, 21s.; l. p. 84s.

ALGER, J. G., *Englishmen in the French Revolution*, 7s. 6d.

Amateur Angler in Dove Dale, a three weeks' holiday, by E. M. 1s. 6d., 1s. and 5s.

ANDERSEN, H. C., *Fairy Tales*, illust. in colour by E. V. B. 25s., new edit. 5s.

—— *Fairy Tales*, illust. by Scandinavian artists, 6s.

ANDERSON, W., *Pictorial Arts of Japan*, 4 parts, 168s.; artist's proofs, 252s.

ANDRES, *Varnishes, Lacquers, Siccatives, & Sealing-wax*, 12s. 6d.

Angler's strange Experiences, by Cotswold Isys, new edit., 3s. 6d.

ANNESLEY, C., *Standard Opera Glass*, the plots of eighty operas, 3rd edit., 2s. 6d.

Annual American Catalogue of Books, 1886-89, each 10s. 6d., half morocco, 14s.

—— 1890, cloth, 15s., half morocco, cloth sides, 18s.

Antipodean Notes ; a nine months' tour, by Wanderer, 7s. 6d.

APPLETON, *European Guide,* new edit., 2 parts, 10s. each.

ARCHER, W., *English Dramatists of To-day,* 8s. 6d.

ARLOT'S *Coach Painting,* from the French by A. A. Fesquet, 6s.

ARMYTAGE, Hon. Mrs., *Wars of Queen Victoria's Reign,* 5s.

ARNOLD, E., *Birthday Book ;* by Kath. L. and Constance Arnold, 4s. 6d.

—— E. L. L., *Summer Holiday in Scandinavia,* 10s. 6d.

—— *On the Indian Hills, Coffee Planting, &c.,* 2 vols. 24s.

—— R., *Ammonia and Ammonium Compounds,* illust. 5s.

Artistic Japan, text, woodcuts, and coloured plates, vols. I.-VI., 15s. each.

ASBJÖRNSEN, P. C., *Round the Yule Log,* 7s. 6d. ; new edit. 5s.

ASHE, R. P., *Two Kings of Uganda ;* six years in Eastern Equatorial Africa, 6s. ; new edit. 3s. 6d.

—— *Uganda, England's latest Charge,* stiff cover, 1s.

ASHTON, F. T., *Designing fancy Cotton and Woollen Cloths,* illust. 50s.

ATCHISON, C. C., *Winter Cruise in Summer Seas ;* "how I found" health, 16s.

ATKINSON, J. B. *Overbeck.* See Great Artists.

ATTWELL, *Italian Masters,* especially in the National Gallery, 3s. 6d.

AUDSLEY, G. A., *Chromolithography,* 44 coloured plates and text, 63s.

—— *Ornamental Arts of Japan,* 2 vols. morocco, 23l. 2s. ; four parts, 15l. 15s.

—— W. and G. A., *Ornament in all Styles,* 31s. 6d.

AUERBACH, B., *Brigitta* (B. Tauchnitz), 2s. ; sewed, 1s. 6d.

—— *On the Height* (B. Tauchnitz), 3 vols. 6s. ; sewed, 4s. 6d.

—— *Spinoza* (B. Tauchnitz), 2 vols. 4s.

AUSTRALIA. See F.Countries.

AUSTRIA. See F. Countries.

Autumn Cruise in the Ægean, by one of the party. See "Fitzpatrick."

BACH. See Great Musicians.

BACON. See English Philosophers.

—— DELIA, *Biography,* 10s. 6d.

BADDELEY, W. St. Clair, *Love's Vintage ;* sonnets and lyrics, 5s.

—— *Tchay and Chianti,* a short visit to Russia and Finland, 5s.

—— *Travel-tide,* 7s. 6d.

BAKER, James, *John Westacott,* new edit. 6s. and 3s. 6d.

BALDWIN, J., *Story of Siegfried,* illust. 6s.

—— *Story of Roland,* illust. 6s.

—— *Story of the Golden Age,* illust. 6s.

—— J. D., *Ancient America,* illust. 10s. 6d.

Ballad Stories. See Bayard Series.

Ballads of the Cid, edited by Rev. Gerrard Lewis, 3s. 6d.

BALLANTYNE, T., *Essays.* See Bayard Series.

BALLIN, ADA S., *Science of Dress*, illust. 6s.

BAMFORD, A. J., *Turbans and Tails*, 7s. 6d.

BANCROFT, G., *History of America*, new edit. 6 vols. 73s. 6d.

Barbizon Painters, by J. W. Mollett—I. Millet, T. Rousseau, and Diaz, 3s. 6d. II. Corot, Daubigny and Dupré, 3s. 6d.; the two in one vol. 7s. 6d.

BARING-GOULD. See Foreign Countries.

BARLOW, A., *Weaving*, new edit. 25s.

—— P. W., *Kaipara, New Z.*, 6s.

—— W., *Matter and Force*, 12s.

BARRETT. See Gr. Musicians.

BARROW, J., *Mountain Ascents*, new edit. 5s.

BASSETT, *Legends of the Sea*, 7s. 6d.

BATHGATE, A., *Waitaruna, New Zealand*, 5s.

Bayard Series, edited by the late J. Hain Friswell; flexible cloth extra, 2s. 6d. each.

Chevalier Bayard, by Berville.
De Joinville, St. Louis.
Essays of Cowley.
Abdallah, by Laboullaye.
Table-Talk of Napoleon.
Vathek, by Beckford.
Cavalier and Puritan Songs.
Words of Wellington.
Johnson's Rasselas.
Hazlitt's Round Table.
Browne's Religio Medici.
Ballad Stories of the Affections, by Robert Buchanan.
Coleridge's Christabel, &c.
Chesterfield's Letters.
Essays in Mosaic, by T. Ballantyne.
My Uncle Toby.
Rochefoucauld, Reflections.
Socrates, Memoirs from Xenophon.
Prince Albert's Precepts.

BEACONSFIELD, *Public Life*, 3s. 6d.

—— See also Prime Ministers.

BEAUGRAND, *Young Naturalists*, new edit. 5s.

BECKER, A.L., *First German Book*, 1s.; *Exercises*, 1s.; *Key to both*, 2s. 6d.; *German Idioms*, 1s. 6d.

BECKFORD. See Bayard Series.

BEECHER, H. W., *Biography*, new edit. 10s. 6d.

BEETHOVEN. See Great Musicians.

BEHNKE, E., *Child's Voice*, 3s. 6d.

BELL, *Obeah, Witchcraft in the West Indies*, 2s. 6d.

BELLENGER & WITCOMB'S French and English Conversations, new edit. Paris, bds. 2s.

BENJAMIN, *Atlantic Islands as health, &c., resorts*. 16s.

BERLIOZ. See Gr. Musicians.

BERVILLE. See Bayard Series.

BIART, *Young Naturalist*, new edit. 7s. 6d.

—— *Involuntary Voyage*, 7s. 6d. and 5s.

—— *Two Friends*, translated by Mary de Hauteville, 7s. 6d. See also Low's Standard Books.

BICKERSTETH, ASHLEY, B.A., *Outlines of Roman History*, 2s. 6d.

—— E. H., Exon., *Clergyman in his Home*, 1s.

—— *From Year to Year*, original poetical pieces, morocco or calf, 10s. 6d.; padded roan, 6s.; roan, 5s.; cloth, 3s. 6d.

—— *Hymnal Companion*, full lists post free.

—— *Master's Home Call*, new edit. 1s.

—— *Octave of Hymns*, sewn, 3d., with music, 1s.

BICKERSTETH, E. H., Exon., *Reef, Parables, &c.,* illust. **7s. 6d.** and **2s. 6d.**

—— *Shadowed Home,* n. ed. **5s.**

BIGELOW, JOHN, *France and the Confederate Navy,* an international episode, **7s. 6d.**

BILBROUGH, *'Twixt France and Spain,* **7s. 6d.**

BILLROTH, *Care of the Sick,* **6s.**

BIRD, F. J., *Dyer's Companion,* **42s.**

—— F. S., *Land of Dykes and Windmills,* **12s. 6d.**

—— H. E., *Chess Practice,* **2s. 6d.**

BISHOP. See Nursing Record Series.

BLACK, ROBERT, *Horse Racing in France,* **14s.**

—— W., *Donald Ross of Heimra,* 3 vols. **31s. 6d.**

—— Novels, new and uniform edition in monthly vols. **2s. 6d.** ea.

—— See Low's Standard Novels.

BLACKBURN, C. F., *Catalogue Titles, Index Entries, &c.* **14s.**

—— H., *Art in the Mountains,* new edit. **5s.**

—— *Artists and Arabs,* **7s 6d.**

—— *Breton Folk,* new issue, **10s. 6d.**

—— *Harz Mountains,* **12s.**

—— *Normandy Picturesque,* **16s.**

—— *Pyrenees,* illust. by Gustave Doré, new edit. **7s. 6d.**

BLACKMORE, R. D., *Georgics,* **4s. 6d.**; cheap edit. **1s.**

—— *Lorna Doone, édit. de luxe,* **35s.**, **31s. 6d.** & **21s.**

—— *Lorna Doone,* illust. by W. Small, **7s. 6d.**

—— *Springhaven,* illust. **12s.**; new edit. **7s. 6d.** & **6s.**

—— See also Low's Standard Novels.

BLAIKIE, *How to get Strong,* new edit. **5s.**

—— *Sound Bodies for our Boys and Girls,* **2s. 6d.**

BLOOMFIELD. See Choice Editions.

Bobby, a Story, by Vesper, **1s.**

BOCK, *Head Hunters of Borneo,* **36s.**

—— *Temples & Elephants,* **21s.**

BONAPARTE, MAD. PATTERSON, *Life,* **10s. 6d.**

BONWICK, JAMES, *Colonial Days,* **2s. 6d.**

—— *Colonies,* **1s.** ea.; 1 vol. **5s.**

—— *Daily Life of the Tasmanians,* **12s. 6d.**

—— *First Twenty Years of Australia,* **5s.**

—— *Last of the Tasmanians,* **16s.**

—— *Port Philip,* **21s.**

—— *Lost Tasmanian Race,* **4s.**

BOSANQUET, C., *Blossoms from the King's Garden,* **6s.**

—— *Jehoshaphat,* **1s.**

—— *Lenten Meditations,* I. **1s. 6d.**; II. **2s.**

—— *Tender Grass for Lambs,* **2s. 6d.**

BOULTON, N. W. *Rebellions,* Canadian life, **9s.**

BOURKE, *On the Border with Crook,* illust., roy. 8vo, **21s.**

—— *Snake Dance of Arizona,* **21s.**

BOUSSENARD. See Low's Standard Books.

BOWEN, F., *Modern Philosophy,* new ed. **16s.**

BOWER. See English Philosophers.

—— *Law of Electric Lighting,* **12s. 6d.**

BOYESEN, H. H., *Against Heavy Odds,* **5s.**

—— *History of Norway,* **7s. 6d.**

BOYESEN, *Modern Vikings*, 6*s.*
Boy's *Froissart, King Arthur, Mabinogian, Percy,* see "Lanier."
BRADSHAW, *New Zealand as it is*, 12*s.* 6*d.*
—— *New Zealand of To-day*, 14*s.*
BRANNT, *Fats and Oils*, 35*s.*
—— *Soap and Candles*, 35*s.*
—— *Vinegar, Acetates*, 25*s.*
—— *Distillation of Alcohol*, 12*s.* 6*d.*
—— *Metal Worker's Receipts*, 12*s.* 6*d.*
—— *Metallic Alloys*, 12*s.* 6*d.*
—— and WAHL, *Techno-Chemical Receipt Book*, 10*s.* 6*d.*
BRASSEY, LADY, *Tahiti*, 21*s.*
BRÉMONT. See Low's Standard Novels.
BRETON, JULES, *Life of an Artist*, an autobiography, 7*s.* 6*d.*
BRISSE, *Menus and Recipes*, new edit. 5*s.*
Britons in Brittany, by G. H. F. 2*s.* 6*d.*
BROCK-ARNOLD. See Great Artists.
BROOKS, NOAH, *Boy Settlers*, 6*s.*
BROWN, A. J., *Rejected of Men*, 3*s.* 6*d.*
—— A. S. *Madeira and Canary Islands for Invalids*, 2*s.* 6*d.*
—— *Northern Atlantic*, for travellers, 4*s.* 6*d.*
—— ROBERT. See Low's Standard Novels.
BROWNE, LENNOX, and BEHNKE, *Voice, Song, & Speech*, 15*s.*; new edit. 5*s.*
—— *Voice Use*, 3*s.* 6*d.*
—— SIR T. See Bayard Series.
BRYCE, G., *Manitoba*, 7*s.* 6*d.*
—— *Short History of the Canadian People*, 7*s.* 6*d.*

BUCHANAN, R. See Bayard Series.
BULKELEY, OWEN T., *Lesser Antilles*, 2*s.* 6*d.*
BUNYAN. See Low's Standard Series.
BURDETT-COUTTS, *Brookfield Stud*, 5*s.*
BURGOYNE, *Operations in Egypt*, 5*s.*
BURNABY, F. See Low's Standard Library.
—— MRS., *High Alps in Winter*, 14*s.*
BURNLEY, JAMES, *History of Wool*, 21*s.*
BUTLER, COL. SIR W. F., *Campaign of the Cataracts*, 18*s.*
—— *Red Cloud*, 7*s.* 6*d.* & 5*s.*
—— See also Low's Standard Books.
BUXTON, ETHEL M. WILMOT, *Wee Folk*, 5*s.*
—— See also Illust Text Books.
BYNNER. See Low's Standard Novels.
CABLE, G. W., *Bonaventure*, 5*s.*
CADOGAN, LADY A., *Drawing-room Comedies*, illust. 10*s.* 6*d.*, acting edit. 6*d.*
—— *Illustrated Games of Patience*, col. diagrams, 12*s.* 6*d.*
—— *New Games of Patience*, with coloured diagrams, 12*s.* 6*d.*
CAHUN. See Low's Standard Books.
CALDECOTT, RANDOLPH, Memoir, by H. Blackburn, new edit. 7*s.* 6*d.* and 5*s.*
—— *Sketches*, pict. bds. 2*s.* 6*d.*
CALL, ANNIE PAYSON, *Power through Repose*, 3*s.* 6*d.*
CALLAN, H., M.A., *Wanderings on Wheel and Foot through Europe*, 1*s.* 6*d.*
Cambridge Trifles, 2*s.* 6*d.*

Cambridge Staircase, 2s. 6d.

CAMPBELL, LADY COLIN, *Book of the Running Brook*, 5s.

—— T.   See Choice Editions.

CANTERBURY, ARCHBISHOP. See Preachers.

CARLETON, WILL, *City Ballads*, illust. 12s. 6d.

—— *City Legends*, ill. 12s. 6d.

—— *Farm Festivals*, ill. 12s. 6d.

—— See also Rose Library.

CARLYLE, *Irish Journey in 1849*, 7s. 6d.

CARNEGIE, ANDREW, *American Four-in-hand in Britain*, 10s. 6d. ; also 1s.

—— *Round the World*, 10s. 6d.

—— *Triumphant Democracy*, 6s. ; new edit. 1s. 6d.; paper, 1s.

CAROVÉ, *Story without an End*, illust. by E. V. B., 7s. 6d.

Celebrated Racehorses, 4 vols. 126s.

CÉLIÈRE. See Low's Standard Books.

Changed Cross, &c., poems, 2s.6d.

Chant-book Companion to the Common Prayer, 2s. ; organ ed. 4s.

CHAPIN, *Mountaineering in Colorado*, 10s. 6d.

CHAPLIN, J. G., *Bookkeeping*, 2s. 6d.

CHATTOCK, *Notes on Etching* new edit. 10s. 6d.

CHERUBINI.   See Great Musicians.

CHESTERFIELD.   See Bayard Series.

Choice Editions of choice books, illustrated by C. W. Cope, R.A., T. Creswick, R.A., E. Duncan, Birket Foster, J. C. Horsley, A.R.A., G. Hicks, R. Redgrave, R.A., C. Stonehouse, F. Tayler, G. Thomas, H. G. Townsend,

Choice Editions—continued.

E. H. Wehnert, Harrison Weir, &c., cloth extra gilt, gilt edges, 2s. 6d. each ; re-issue, 1s. each Bloomfield's Farmer's Boy.

Campbell's Pleasures of Hope
Coleridge's Ancient Mariner.
Goldsmith's Deserted Village.
Goldsmith's Vicar of Wakefield.
Gray's Elegy in a Churchyard.
Keats' Eve of St. Agnes.
Milton's Allegro.
Poetry of Nature, by H. Weir.
Rogers' Pleasures of Memory.
Shakespeare's Songs and Sonnets.
Elizabethan Songs and Sonnets.
Tennyson's May Queen.
Wordsworth's Pastoral Poems.

CHREIMAN, *Physical Culture of Women*, 1s.

CLARK, A., *A Dark Place of the Earth*, 6s.

—— Mrs. K. M., *Southern Cross Fairy Tale*, 5s.

CLARKE, C. C., *Writers, and Letters*, 10s. 6d.

—— PERCY, *Three Diggers*, 6s.

—— *Valley Council ;* from T. Bateman's Journal, 6s.

Classified Catalogue of English-printed Educational Works, 3rd edit. 6s.

Claude le Lorrain. See Great Artists.

CLOUGH, A. H., *Plutarch's Lives*, one vol. 18s.

COLERIDGE, C. R., *English Squire*, 6s.

—— S. T. See Choice Editions and Bayard Series.

COLLINGWOOD, H. See Low's Standard Books.

COLLINSON, Adm. SIR R., *H.M.S. Enterprise in Search of Franklin*, 14s.

CONDER, J., *Flowers of Japan ; Decoration*, coloured Japanese Plates, 42s. nett.

CORREGGIO. See Great Artists.

COWLEY. See Bayard Series.

COX, DAVID. See Great Artists.

COZZENS, F., *American Yachts*, pfs. 21*l.*; art. pfs. 31*l.* 10*s.*
—— See also Low's Standard Books.

CRADDOCK. See Low's Standard Novels.

CREW, B. J., *Petroleum*, 21*s.*

CRISTIANI, R. S., *Soap and Candles*, 42*s.*
—— *Perfumery*, 25*s.*

CROKER, MRS. B. M. See Low's Standard Novels.

CROUCH, A. P., *Glimpses of Feverland* (West Africa), 6*s.*
—— *On a Surf-bound Coast*, 7*s.* 6*d.*; new edit. 5*s.*

CRUIKSHANK G. See Great Artists.

CUDWORTH, W., *Abraham Sharp*, 26*s.*

CUMBERLAND, STUART, *Thought-reader's Thoughts*,10*s.* 6*d.*
—— See also Low's Standard Novels.

CUNDALL, F. See Great Artists.
—— J., *Shakespeare*, 3*s.* 6*d.*, 5*s.* and 2*s.*

CURTIN, J., *Myths of the Russians*, 10*s.* 6*d.*

CURTIS, C. B., *Velazquez and Murillo*, with etchings, 31*s.* 6*d.* and 63*s.*

CUSHING, W., *Anonyms*, 2 vols. 52*s.* 6*d.*
—— *Initials and Pseudonyms*, 25*s.*; ser. II., 21*s.*

CUTCLIFFE, H. C., *Trout Fishing*, new edit. 3*s.* 6*d.*

DALY, MRS. D., *Digging, Squatting, &c., in N. S. Australia*, 12*s.*

D'ANVERS, N., *Architecture and Sculpture*, new edit. 5*s.*
—— *Elementary Art, Architecture, Sculpture, Painting*, new edit. 10*s.* 6*d.*
—— *Elementary History of Music*, 2*s.* 6*d.*
—— *Painting*, by F. Cundall, 6*s.*

DAUDET, A., *My Brother Jack*, 7*s.* 6*d.*; also 5*s.*
—— *Port Tarascon*, by H. James, 7*s.* 6*d.*; new edit. 5*s.*

DAVIES, C., *Modern Whist*, 4*s.*

DAVIS, C. T., *Bricks, Tiles, &c.*, new edit. 25*s.*
—— *Manufacture of Leather*, 52*s.* 6*d.*
—— *Manufacture of Paper*, 28*s.*
—— *Steam Boiler Incrustation*, 8*s.* 6*d.*
—— G. B., *International Law*, 10*s.* 6*d.*

DAWIDOWSKY, *Glue, Gelatine, &c.*, 12*s.* 6*d.*

Day of my Life, by an Eton boy, new edit. 2*s.* 6*d.*; also 1*s.*

DE JOINVILLE. See Bayard Series.

DE LEON, EDWIN, *Under the Stars and Under the Crescent*, 2 vols. 12*s.*; new edit. 6*s.*

DELLA ROBBIA. See Great Artists.

Denmark and Iceland. See Foreign Countries.

DENNETT, R. E., *Seven Years among the Fjort*, 7*s.* 6*d.*

DERRY (Bishop of). See Preachers.

DE WINT. See Great Artists.

DIGGLE, J. W., *Bishop Fraser's Lancashire Life*, new edit. 12*s.* 6*d.*; popular ed. 3*s.* 6*d.*
—— *Sermons for Daily Life*, 5*s.*

DOBSON, Austin, *Hogarth,*
with a bibliography, &c., of
prints, illust. 24s.; l.paper 52s.6d.
—— See also Great Artists.
DODGE, Mrs., *Hans Brinker,*
the Silver Skates, new edit. 5s.,
3s. 6d.. 2s. 6d. ; text only, 1s.
DONKIN, J. G., *Trooper and*
Redskin ; N. W. mounted police,
Canada, 8s. 6d.
DONNELLY, Ignatius, *Atlan-*
tis, the Antediluvian World, new
edit. 12s. 6d.
—— *Cæsar's Column,* authorized
edition, 3s. 6d.
—— *Doctor Huguet,* 3s. 6d.
—— *Great Cryptogram,* Bacon's
Cipher in Shakespeare, 2 vols.
30s.
—— *Ragnarok : the Age of*
Fire and Gravel, 12s. 6d.
DORÉ, Gustave, *Life and Re-*
miniscences, by Blanche Roose-
velt, fully illust. 24s.
DOS PASSOS, J. R., *Law of*
Stockbrokers and Stock Exchanges,
35s.
DOUDNEY, Sarah, *Godiva*
Durleigh, 3 vols. 31s. 6d.
DOUGALL, J. D., *Shooting*
Appliances, Practice, &c., 10s. 6d.;
new edit. 7s. 6d.
DOUGHTY, H. M., *Friesland*
Meres and the Netherlands, new
edit. illust. 10s. 6d.
DOVETON, F. B., *Poems and*
Snatches of Songs, 5s. ; new edit.
3s. 6d.
DU CHAILLU, Paul. See
Low's Standard Books.
DUNCKLEY ("Verax.") See
Prime Ministers.
DUNDERDALE,   George,
Prairie and Bush, 6s.
Dürer. See Great Artists.
DYKES, J. Oswald.   See
Preachers.

Echoes from the Heart, 3s. 6d.
EDEN, C. H.   See Foreign
Countries.
EDMONDS, C., *Poetry of the*
Anti-Jacobin, new edit. 7s. 6d.
and 21s.
Educational Catalogue.   See
Classified Catalogue.
EDWARDS, *American Steam*
Engineer, 12s. 6d.
—— *Modern Locomotive En-*
gines, 12s. 6d.
—— *Steam Engineer's Guide,*
12s. 6d.
—— H. Sutherland.   See
Great Musicians.
—— M. B., *Dream of Millions,*
&c., 1s.
—— See Low's Standard Novels.
EGGLESTON, G. Cary, *Jug-*
gernaut, 6s.
Egypt.   See Foreign Countries.
Elizabethan Songs.   See Choice
Editions.
EMERSON, Dr. P. H., *East*
Coast Yarns, 1s.
—— *English Idylls,* new ed. 2s.
—— *Naturalistic Photography,*
new edit. 5s.
—— *Pictures of East Anglian*
Life ; plates and vignettes, 105s.
and 147s.
—— and GOODALL, *Life on*
the Norfolk Broads, plates, 126s.
and 210s.
—— *Wild Life on a Tidal*
Water, copper plates, ord. edit.
25s. ; *édit. de luxe,* 63s.
—— R. W., by G. W. COOKE,
8s. 6d.
—— *Birthday Book,* 3s. 6d.
—— *In Concord,* a memoir,
7s. 6d.
English Catalogue, 1863-71,
42s. ; 1872-80, 42s. ; 1881-9,
52s. 6d. ; 5s. yearly.

English Catalogue, Index vol. 1837-56, 26s.; 1856-76, 42s.; 1874-80, 18s.

—— Etchings, vol. v. 45s.; vi., 25s.; vii., 25s.; viii., 42s.

English Philosophers, edited by E. B. Ivan Müller, M.A., 3s. 6d. each.
Bacon, by Fowler.
Hamilton, by Monck.
Hartley and James Mill, by Bower.
Shaftesbury & Hutcheson; Fowler.
Adam Smith, by J. A. Farrer.

ERCKMANN-CHATRIAN. See Low's Standard Books.

ERICHSON, Life, by W. C. Church, 2 vols. 24s.

ESMARCH, F., Handbook of Surgery, 24s.

Essays on English Writers. See Gentle Life Series.

EVANS, G. E., Repentance of Magdalene Despar, &c., poems, 5s.

—— S. & F., Upper Ten, a story, 1s.

—— W. E., Songs of the Birds, n. ed. 6s.

EVELYN, J., An Inca Queen, 5s.

—— JOHN, Life of Mrs. Godolphin, 7s. 6d.

EVES, C. W., West Indies, n. ed. 7s. 6d.

FAIRBAIRN, A. M. See Preachers.

Familiar Words. See Gentle Life Series.

FARINI, G. A., Kalahari Desert, 21s.

FARRAR, C. S., History of Sculpture, &c., 6s.

—— MAURICE, Minnesota, 6s.

FAURIEL, Last Days of the Consulate, 10s. 6d.

FAY, T., Three Germanys, 2 vols. 35s.

FEILDEN, H. St. J., Some Public Schools, 2s. 6d.

—— Mrs., My African Home, 7s. 6d.

FENN, G. MANVILLE. See Low's Standard Books.

FENNELL, J. G., Book of the Roach, n. ed. 2s.

FFORDE, B., Subaltern, Policeman, and the Little Girl. 1s.

—— Trotter, a Poona Mystery, 1s.

FIELD, MAUNSELL B., Memories, 10s. 6d.

FIELDS, JAMES T., Memoirs, 12s. 6d.

—— Yesterdays with Authors, 16s.; also 10s. 6d.

Figure Painters of Holland. See Great Artists.

FINCK, HENRY T., Pacific Coast Scenic Tour, 10s. 6d.

FITCH, LUCY. See Nursing Record Series, 1s.

FITZGERALD. See Foreign Countries.

—— PERCY, Book Fancier, 5s. and 12s. 6d

FITZPATRICK, T., Autumn Cruise in the Ægean, 10s. 6d

—— Transatlantic Holiday, 10s. 6d.

FLEMING, S., England and Canada, 6s.

Foreign Countries and British Colonies, descriptive handbooks edited by F. S. Pulling, M.A. Each volume is the work of a writer who has special acquaintance with the subject, 3s. 6d.
Australia. by Fitzgerald.
Austria-Hungary, by Kay.
Denmark and Iceland, by E. C. Otté.
Egypt, by S. L. Poole.
France, by Miss Roberts.
Germany, by L. Sergeant.
Greece, by S. Baring Gould.

Foreign Countries, &c.—cont.
Japan, by Mossman.
Peru, by R. Markham.
Russia, by Morfill.
Spain, by Webster.
Sweden and Norway, by Woods.
West Indies, by O. H. Eden.

FOREMAN, J., *Philippine Islands*, 21*s.*

FOTHERINGHAM, L. M., *Nyassaland*, 7*s.* 6*d.*

FOWLER, *Japan, China, and India*, 10*s.* 6*d.*

FRA ANGELICO. See Great Artists.

FRA BARTOLOMMEO, AL-BERTINELLI, and ANDREA DEL SARTO. See Great Artists.

FRANC, MAUD JEANNE, *Beatrice Melton*, 4*s.*
—— *Emily's Choice*, n. ed. 5*s.*
—— *Golden Gifts*, 4*s.*
—— *Hall's Vineyard*, 4*s.*
—— *Into the Light*, 4*s.*
—— *John's Wife*, 4*s.*
—— *Little Mercy; for better, for worse*, 4*s.*
—— *Marian, a Tale*, n. ed. 5*s.*
—— *Master of Ralston*, 4*s.*
—— *Minnie's Mission, a Temperance Tale*, 4*s.*
—— *No longer a Child*, 4*s.*
—— *Silken Cords and Iron Fetters, a Tale*, 4*s.*
—— *Two Sides to Every Question*, 4*s.*
—— *Vermont Vale*, 5*s.*
A plainer edition is published at 2*s.* 6*d.*

France. See Foreign Countries.

FRANCIS, F., *War, Waves, and.Wanderings*, 2 vols. 24*s.*
—— See also Low's Standard Series.

Frank's Ranche; or, My Holiday in the Rockies, n. ed. 5*s.*

FRANKEL, JULIUS, *Starch Glucose, &c.*, 18*s.*

FRASER, BISHOP, *Lancashire Life*, n. ed. 12*s.* 6*d.*; popular ed. 3*s.* 6*d.*

FREEMAN, J., *Melbourne Life, lights and shadows*, 6*s.*

FRENCH, F., *Home Fairies and Heart Flowers.* illust. 24*s.*

French and English Birthday Book, by Kate D. Clark, 7*s.* 6*d.*

French Revolution, Letters from Paris, translated, 10*s.* 6*d.*

Fresh Woods and Pastures New, by the Author of "An Angler's Days," 5*s.*, 1*s.* 6*d.*, 1*s.*

FRIEZE, *Duprè, Florentine Sculptor*, 7*s.* 6*d.*

FRISWELL, J. H. See Gentle Life Series.

Froissart for Boys, by Lanier, new ed. 7*s.* 6*d.*

FROUDE, J. A. See Prime Ministers.

Gainsborough and Constable. See Great Artists.

GASPARIN, *Sunny Fields and Shady Woods*, 6*s.*

GEFFCKEN, *British Empire*, 7*s.* 6*d.*

Generation of Judges, n.e. 7*s.*6*d.*

Gentle Life Series, edited by J. Hain Friswell, sm. 8vo. 6*s.* per vol.; calf extra, 10*s.* 6*d.* ea.; 16mo, 2*s.* 6*d.*, except when price is given.
Gentle Life.
About in the World.
Like unto Christ.
Familiar Words, 6*s.*; also 3*s.* 6*d.*
Montaigne's Essays.
Sidney's Arcadia, 6*s.*
Gentle Life, second series.
Varia; readings, 10*s.* 6*d.*
Silent hour; essays.
Half-length Portraits.
Essays on English Writers.
Other People's Windows, 6*s.* & 2*s.* 6*d.*
A Man's Thoughts.

George Eliot, by G. W. Cooke, 10*s*. 6*d*.

Germany. See Foreign Countries.

GESSI, ROMOLO PASHA, *Seven Years in the Soudan*, 18*s*.

GHIBERTI & DONATELLO. See Great Artists.

GILES, E., *Australia Twice Traversed*, 1872-76, 2 vols. 30*s*.

GILL, J. See Low's Readers.

GILLESPIE, W. M., *Surveying*, n. ed. 21*s*.

Giotto, by Harry Quilter, illust. 15*s*.

—— See also Great Artists.

GIRDLESTONE, C., *Private Devotions*, 2*s*.

GLADSTONE. See Prime Ministers.

GLENELG, P., *Devil and the Doctor*, 1*s*.

GLOVER, R., *Light of the World*, n. ed., 2*s*. 6*d*.

GLÜCK. See Great Musicians.

Goethe's Faustus, in orig. rhyme, by Huth, 5*s*.

—— *Prosa*, by C. A. Buchheim (Low's German Series), 3*s*. 6*d*.

GOLDSMITH, O., *She Stoops to Conquer*, by Austin Dobson, illust. by E. A. Abbey, 84*s*.

—— See also Choice Editions.

GOOCH, FANNY C., *Mexicans*, 16*s*.

GOODALL, *Life and Landscape on the Norfolk Broads*, 126*s*. and 210*s*.

—— &EMERSON, *Pictures of East Anglian Life*, £5 5*s*. and £7 7*s*.

GOODMAN, E. J., *The Best Tour in Norway*, 6*s*.

—— N. & A., *Fen Skating*, 5*s*.

GOODYEAR, W. H., *Grammar of the Lotus, Ornament and Sun Worship*, 63*s*. nett.

GORDON, J. E. H., *Physical Treatise on Electricity and Magnetism.* 3rd ed. 2 vols. 42*s*.

—— *Electric Lighting*, 18*s*.

—— *School Electricity*, 5*s*.

—— Mrs. J. E. H., *Decorative Electricity*, illust. 12*s*.

GOWER, LORD RONALD, *Handbook to the Art Galleries of Belgium and Holland*, 5*s*.

—— *Northbrook Gallery*, 63*s*. and 105*s*.

—— *Portraits at Castle Howard.* 2 vols. 126*s*.

—— See also Great Artists.

GRAESSI, *Italian Dictionary*, 3*s*. 6*d*.; roan, 5*s*.

GRAY, T. See Choice Eds.

Great Artists, Biographies, illustrated, emblematical binding, 3*s*. 6*d*. per vol. except where the price is given.

Barbizon School, 2 vols.

Claude le Lorrain.

Correggio, 2*s*. 6*d*.

Cox and De Wint.

George Cruikshank.

Della Robbia and Cellini, 2*s*. 6*d*.

Albrecht Dürer.

Figure Paintings of Holland.

Fra Angelico, Masaccio, &c.

Fra Bartolommeo, &c.

Gainsborough and Constable.

Ghiberti and Donatello, 2*s*. 6*d*.

Giotto, by H. Quilter, 15*s*.

Hogarth, by A. Dobson.

Hans Holbein.

Landscape Painters of Holland.

Landseer.

Leonardo da Vinci.

Little Masters of Germany, by Scott; *id.* de luxe, 10*s*. 6*d*.

Mantegna and Francia.

Meissonier, 2*s*. 6*d*.

Michelangelo.

Mulready.

Murillo, by Minor, 2*s*. 6*d*.

Overbeck.

Raphael.

Great Artists—continued.
Rembrandt.
Reynolds.
Romney and Lawrence, 2s. 6d.
Rubens, by Kett.
Tintoretto, by Osler.
Titian, by Heath.
Turner, by Monkhouse.
Vandyck and Hals.
Velasques.
Vernet & Delaroche.
Watteau, by Mollett, 2s. 6d.
Wilkie, by Mollett.
Great Musicians, edited by
F. Hueffer. A series of bio-
graphies, 3s. each :—
Bach, by Poole.
Beethoven.
*Berlioz.
Cherubini.
English Church Composers,
*Glück.
Handel.
Haydn.
*Marcello.
Mendelssohn.
Mozart.
*Palestrina and the Roman School.
Purcell.
Rossini and Modern Italian School.
Schubert.
Schumann.
Richard Wagner.
Weber.
* *Are not yet published.*
Greece. See Foreign Countries.
GRIEB, *German Dictionary*, n.
ed. 2 vols. 21s.
GRIMM, H., *Literature*, 8s. 6d.
GROHMANN, *Camps in the
Rockies*, 12s. 6d.
GROVES, J. Percy. See
Low's Standard Books.
GUIZOT, *History of England*,
illust. 3 vols. re-issue at 10s. 6d.
per vol.
—— *History of France*, illust.
re-issue, 8 vols. 10s. 6d. each.
—— Abridged by G. Masson, 5s.
GUYON, Madame, *Life*, 6s.

HADLEY, J., *Roman Law*,
7s. 6d.
Half-length Portraits. See
Gentle Life Series.
HALFORD, F. M., *Dry Fly-
fishing*, n. ed. 25s.
—— *Floating Flies*, 15s. & 30s.
HALL, *How to Live Long*, 2s.
HALSEY, F. A., *Slide Valve
Gears*, 8s. 6d.
HAMILTON. See English
Philosophers.
—— E. *Fly-fishing*, 6s. and
10s. 6d.
—— *Riverside Naturalist*, 14s.
HAMILTON'S *Mexican Hand-
book*, 8s. 6d.
HANDEL. See Great Musi-
cians.
HANDS, T:, *Numerical Exer-
cises in Chemistry*, 2s. 6d. ; with-
out ans. 2s. ; ans. sep. 6d.
Handy Guide to Dry-fly Fishing,
by Cotswold Isys, 1s.
*Handy Guide Book to Japanese
Islands*, 6s. 6d.
HARDY, A. S., *Passe-rose*, 6s.
—— Thos. See Low's Stand-
ard Novels.
HARKUT, F., *Conspirator*, 6s.
HARLAND, Marion, *Home
Kitchen*, 5s.
Harper's Young People, vols.
I.—VII. 7s. 6d. each ; gilt 8s.
HARRIES, A. See Nursing
Record Series.
HARRIS, W. B., *Land of the
African Sultan*, 10s. 6d. ; l. p.
31s. 6d.
HARRISON, Mary, *Modern
Cookery*, 6s.
—— *Skilful Cook*, n. ed. 5s.
—— Mrs. B. *Old-fashioned
Fairy Book*, 6s.
—— W., *London Houses*, Illust.
n. edit. 1s. 6d., 6s. net ; & 2s. 6d.

HARTLEY and MILL. See English Philosophers.

HATTON, JOSEPH, *Journalistic London*, 12*s.* 6*d.*

—— See also Low's Standard Novels.

HAWEIS, H.R., *Broad Church*, 6*s.*

—— *Poets in the Pulpit,* 10*s.* 6*d.* new edit. 6*s.*; also 3*s.* 6*d.*

—— Mrs., *Housekeeping*, 2*s.* 6*d.*

—— *Beautiful Houses*, 4*s.*, new edit. 1*s.*

HAYDN. See Great Musicians.

HAZLITT, W., *Round Table*, 2*s.* 6*d.*

HEAD, PERCY R. See Illus. Text Books and Great Artists.

HEARD, A.F., *Russian Church*, 16*s.*

HEARN, L., *Youma*, 5*s.*

HEATH, F. G., *Fern World*, 12*s.* 6*d.*, new edit. 6*s.*

—— GERTRUDE, *Tell us Why*, 2*s.* 6*d.*

HELDMANN, B., *Mutiny of the " Leander,"* 7*s.* 6*d.* and 5*s.*

—— See also Low's Standard Books for Boys.

HENTY, G. A., *Hidden Foe*, 2 vols. 21*s.*

—— See also Low's Standard Books for Boys.

—— RICHMOND, *Australiana*, 5*s.*

HERBERT, T., *Salads and Sandwiches*, 6*d.*

HICKS, C. S., *Our Boys, and what to do with Them; Merchant Service*, 5*s.*

—— *Yachts, Boats, and Canoes*, 10*s.* 6*d.*

HIGGINSON, T. W., *Atlantic Essays*, 6*s.*

—— *History of the U.S.*, illust. 14*s.*

HILL, A. STAVELEY, *From Home to Home in N.-W. Canada*, 21*s.*, new edit. 7*s.* 6*d.*

—— G. B., *Footsteps of Johnson*, 63*s.*; *édition de luxe*, 147*s.*

HINMAN, R., *Eclectic Physical Geography*, 5*s.*

Hints on proving Wills without Professional Assistance, n. ed. 1*s.*

HOEY, Mrs. CASHEL. See Low's Standard Novels.

HOFFER, *Caoutchouc & Gutta Percha*, 12*s.* 6*d.*

HOGARTH. See Gr. Artists.

HOLBEIN. See Great Artists.

HOLDER, CHARLES F., *Ivory King*, 8*s.* 6*d.*

—— *Living Lights*, 8*s.* 6*d.*

—— *Marvels of Animal Life*, 8*s.* 6*d.*

HOLM, SAXE, *Draxy Miller*, 2*s.* 6*d.* and 2*s.*

HOLMES, O. WENDELL, *Before the Curfew*, 5*s.*

—— *Over the Tea Cups*, 6*s.*

—— *Iron Gate, &c., Poems*, 6*s.*

—— *Last Leaf*, 42*s.*

—— *Mechanism in Thought and Morals*, 1*s.* 6*d.*

—— *Mortal Antipathy*, 8*s.* 6*d.*, 2*s.* and 1*s.*

—— *Our Hundred Days in Europe*, new edit. 6*s.*; l. paper 15*s.*

—— *Poetical Works*, new edit., 2 vols. 10*s.* 6*d.*

—— *Works*, prose, 10 vols.; poetry, 4 vols.; 14 vols. 84*s.* Limited large paper edit., 14 vols. 294*s.* nett.

—— See also Low's Standard Novels and Rose Library.

HOLUB, E., *South Africa*, 2 vols. 42*s.*

HOPKINS, MANLEY, *Treatise on the Cardinal Numbers*, 2*s.* 6*d.*

Horace in Latin, with Smart's literal translation, 2s. 6d.; translation only, 1s. 6d.

HORETZKY, C., *Canada on the Pacific*, 5s.

How and where to Fish in Ireland, by H. Regan, 3s. 6d.

HOWARD, BLANCHE W., *Tony the Maid*, 3s. 6d.

—— See also Low's Standard Novels.

HOWELLS, W. D., *Suburban Sketches*, 7s. 6d.

—— *Undiscovered Country*, 3s. 6d. and 1s.

HOWORTH, H. H., *Glacial Nightmare*, 18s.

—— *Mammoth and the Flood*, 18s.

HUDSON, N. H., *Purple Land that England Lost;* Banda Oriental 2 vols. 21s.: 1 vol. 6s.

HUEFFER. E. See Great Musicians.

HUGHES, HUGH PRICE. See Preachers.

HUME, F., *Creature of the Night*, 1s.

Humorous Art at the Naval Exhibition, 1s.

HUMPHREYS, JENNET, *Some Little Britons in Brittany*, 2s. 6d.

Hundred Greatest Men, new edit. one vol. 21s.

HUNTINGDON, *The Squire's Nieces*, 2s. 6d. (Playtime Library.)

HYDE, *Hundred Years by Post*, 1s.

Hymnal Companion to the Book of Common Prayer, separate lists gratis.

Iceland. See Foreign Countries.

Illustrated Text-Books of Art-Education, edit. by E. J. Poynter, R.A., illust. 5s. each.

Architecture, Classic and Early Christian.

Illust. Text-Books—continued.

Architecture, Gothic and Renaissance.

German, Flemish, and Dutch Painting.

Painting, Classic and Italian.

Painting, English and American.

Sculpture, modern.

Sculpture, by G. Redford.

Spanish and French artists.

INDERWICK, F. A., *Interregnum*, 10s. 6d.

—— *Sidelights on the Stuarts*, new edit. 7s. 6d.

INGELOW, JEAN. See Low's Standard Novels.

INGLIS, *Our New Zealand Cousins*, 6s.

—— *Sport and Work on the Nepaul Frontier*, 21s.

—— *Tent Life in Tiger Land*, 18s.

IRVING, W., *Little Britain*, 10s. 6d. and 6s.

—— *Works*, "Geoffrey Crayon" edit. 27 vols. 16l. 16s.

JACKSON, J., *Handwriting in Relation to Hygiene*, 3d.

—— *New Style Vertical Writing Copy-Books*, Series 1. 1—8, 2d. and 1d. each.

—— *New Code Copy-Books*, 22 Nos. 2d. each.

—— *Shorthand of Arithmetic*, Companion to all Arithmetics, 1s. 6d.

—— L., *Ten Centuries of European Progress*, with maps, 12s. 6d.

JAMES, CROAKE, *Law and Lawyers*, new edit. 7s. 6d.

—— HENRY. See Daudet, A.

JAMES and MOLE'S *French Dictionary*, 3s. 6d. cloth; roan, 5s.

JAMES, *German Dictionary*, 3s. 6d. cloth; roan 5s.

JANVIER, *Aztec Treasure House*, 7s. 6d.; new edit. 5s.

Japan. See Foreign Countries.

JEFFERIES, RICHARD, *Amaryllis at the Fair*, 7s. 6d.

—— *Bevis*, new edit. 5s.

JEPHSON, A. J. M., *Emin Pasha relief expedition*, 21s.

JERDON. See Low's Standard Series.

JOHNSTON, H. H., *The Congo*, 21s.

JOHNSTON-LAVIS, H. J., *South Italian Volcanoes*, 15s.

JOHNSTONE, D. L., *Land of the Mountain Kingdom*, new edit. 3s. 6d. and 2s. 6d.

JONES, MRS. HERBERT, *Sandringham, Past and Present*, illust., new edit. 8s. 6d.

JULIEN, F., *Conversational French Reader*, 2s. 6d.

—— *English Student's French Examiner*, 2s.

—— *First Lessons in Conversational French Grammar*, n. ed. 1s.

—— *French at Home and at School*, Book I. accidence, 2s.; key, 3s.

—— *Petites Leçons de Conversation et de Grammaire*, n. ed. 3s.

—— *Petites Leçons*, with phrases, 3s. 6d.

—— *Phrases of Daily Use*, separately, 6d.

KARR, H. W. SETON, *Shores and Alps of Alaska*, 16s.

KARSLAND, VEVA, *Women and their Work*, 1s.

KAY. See Foreign Countries.

KENNEDY, E. B., *Blacks and Bushrangers*, new edit. 5s., 3s. 6d. and 2s. 6d.

KERR, W. M., *Far Interior, the Cape, Zambesi*, &c., 2 vols. 32s.

KERSHAW, S. W., *Protestants from France in their English Home*, 6s.

KETT, C. W., *Rubens*, 3s. 6d.

Khedives and Pashas, 7s. 6d.

KILNER, E. A., *Four Welsh Counties*, 5s.

King and Commons. See Cavalier in Bayard Series.

KINGSLEY, R. G., *Children of Westminster Abbey*, 5s.

KINGSTON. See Low's Standard Books.

KIPLING, RUDYARD, *Soldiers Three*, &c., stories, 1s.

—— *Story of the Gadsbys*, new edit. 1s.

—— *In Black and White*, &c., stories, 1s.

—— *Wee Willie Winkie*, &c., stories, 1s.

—— *Under the Deodars*, &c., stories, 1s.

—— *Phantom Rickshaw*, &c., stories, 1s.

** The six collections of stories may also be had in 2 vols. 3s. 6d. each.

—— *Stories*, Library Edition, 2 vols. 6s. each.

KIRKALDY, W. G., *David Kirkaldy's Mechanical Testing*. 84s.

KNIGHT, A. L., *In the Web of Destiny*, 7s. 6d.

—— E. F., *Cruise of the Falcon*, new edit. 3s. 6d.

—— E. J., *Albania and Montenegro*, 12s. 6d.

—— V. C., *Church Unity*, 5s.

KNOX, T. W., *Boy Travellers*, new edit. 5s.

KNOX-LITTLE, W. J., *Sermons*, 3s. 6d.

KUNHARDT, C. P., *Small Yachts*, new edit. 50s.

—— *Steam Yachts*, 16s.

KWONG, *English Phrases*, 21s.

LABOULLAYE, E., *Abdallah*, 2s. 6d.

LALANNE, *Etching*, 12s. 6d.

LAMB, CHAS., *Essays of Elia,*
with designs by C. O. Murray, 6*s.*
LAMBERT, *Angling Litera-*
ture, 3*s.* 6*d.*
Landscape Painters of Holland.
See Great Artists.
LANDSEER. See Great Ar-
tists.
LANGLEY, S. P., *New Astro-*
nomy, 10*s.* 6*d.*
LANIER, S., *Boy's Froissart,*
7*s.* 6*d.* ; *King Arthur,* 7*s.* 6*d.* ;
Mabinogion, 7*s.* 6*d.* ; *Percy,* 7*s.* 6*d.*
LANSDELL, HENRY, *Through*
Siberia, 1 v. 15*s.* and 10*s.* 6*d.*
—— *Russia in Central Asia,*
2 vols. 42*s.*
—— *Through Central Asia,* 12*s.*
LARDEN, W., *School Course*
on Heat, n. ed. 5*s.*
LAURIE, A., *Secret of the*
Magian, the Mystery of Ecbatana,
illus. 6*s.* See also Low's Standard
Books.
LAWRENCE, SERGEANT, *Auto-*
biography, 6*s.*
—— and ROMNEY. See Great
Artists.
LAYARD, MRS., *West Indies,*
2*s.* 6*d.*
LEA, H. C., *Inquisition,* 3 vols.
42*s.*
LEARED, A., *Marocco,* n. ed.
16*s.*
LEAVITT, *New World Trage-*
dies, 7*s.* 6*d.*
LEFFINGWELL, W. B.,
Shooting, 18*s.*
—— *Wild Fowl Shooting,*
10*s.* 6*d.*
LEFROY, W., DEAN. See
Preachers.
LELAND, C. G., *Algonquin*
Legends, 8*s.*
LEMON, M., *Small House over*
the Water. 6*s.*

Leo XIII. Life, 18*s.*
Leonardo da Vinci. See Great
Artists.
—— *Literary Works,* by J. P.
Richter, 2 vols. 252*s.*
LIEBER, *Telegraphic Cipher,*
42*s.* nett.
Like unto Christ. See Gentle
Life Series.
LITTLE, ARCH. J., *Yang-tse*
Gorges, n. ed., 10*s.* 6*d.*
Little Masters of Germany. See
Great Artists.
LONGFELLOW, *Miles Stan-*
dish, illus. 21*s.*
—— *Maidenhood,* with col. pl.
2*s.* 6*d.* ; gilt edges, 3*s.* 6*d.*
—— *Nuremberg,* photogr. illu.
31*s.* 6*d.*
—— *Song of Hiawatha,* illust.
21*s.*
LOOMIS, E., *Astronomy,* n. ed.
8*s.* 6*d.*
LORNE, MARQUIS OF, *Canada*
and Scotland, 7*s.* 6*d.*
—— *Palmerston.* See Prime
Ministers.
Louis, St. See Bayard
Series.
Low's French Readers, edit. by
C. F. Clifton, I. 3*d.*, II. 3*d.*, III.
6*d.*
—— *German Series.* See
Goethe, Meissner, Sandars, and
Schiller.
—— *London Charities,* annu-
ally, 1*s.* 6*d.* ; sewed, 1*s.*
—— *Illustrated Germ. Primer,*
1*s.*
—— *Infant Primers,* I. illus.
3*d.* ; II. illus. 6*d.* and 7*d.*.
—— *Pocket Encyclopædia,* with
plates, 3*s.* 6*d.* ; roan, 4*s.* 6*d.*
—— *Readers,* I., 9*d.* ; II., 10*d.* ;
III., 1*s.* ; IV., 1*s.* 3*d.* ; V., 1*s.* 4*d.* ;
VI., 1*s.* 6*d.*

Low's Select Parchment Series.

Aldrich (T. B.) Friar Jerome's Beautiful Book, 3*s.* 6*d.*
Lewis (Rev. Gerrard), Ballads of the Cid, 2*s.* 6*d.*
Whittier (J. G.) The King's Missive. 3*s.* 6*d.*

Low's Stand. Library of Travel (except where price is stated), per volume, 7*s.* 6*d.*
1. Butler, Great Lone Land ; also 3*s.* 6*d.*
2. —— Wild North Land.
3. Stanley (H. M.) Coomassie, 3*s.* 6*d.*
4. —— How I Found Livingstone; also 3*s.* 6*d.*
5. —— Through the Dark Continent, 1 vol. illust., 12*s.* 6*d.*; also 3*s.* 6*d.*
8. MacGahan (J. A.) Oxus.
9. Spry, voyage, *Challenger.*
10. Burnaby's Asia Minor, 10*s.* 6*d.*
11. Schweinfurth's Heart of Africa, 2 vols. 15*s.* ; also 3*s.* 6*d.* each.
12. Marshall (W.) Through America.
13. Lansdell (H). Through Siberia, 10*s.* 6*d.*
14. Coote, South by East, 10*s.* 6*d.*
15. Knight, Cruise of the *Falcon,* also 3*s.* 6*d.*
16. Thomson (Joseph) Through Masai Land.
19. Ashe (R. P.) Two Kings of Uganda, 3*s.* 6*d.*

Low's Standard Novels (except where price is stated), 6*s.*

Baker, John Westacott.
Black (W.) Craig Royston.
—— Daughter of Heth.
—— House Boat.
—— In Far Lochaber.
—— In Silk Attire.
—— Kilmeny.
—— Lady Silverdale's Sweetheart.
—— New Prince Fortunatus.
—— Penance of John Logan.
—— Stand Fast, Craig Royston!
—— Sunrise.
—— Three Feathers.

Low's Stand. Novels—continued

Blackmore (R. D.) Alice Lorraine.
—— Christowell.
—— Clara Vaughan.
—— Cradock Nowell.
—— Cripps the Carrier.
—— Ereme, or My Father's Sins.
—— Kit and Kitty.
—— Lorna Doone.
—— Mary Anerley.
—— Sir Thomas Upmore.
—— Springhaven.
Brémont, Gentleman Digger.
Brown (Robert) Jack Abbott's Log.
Bynner, Agnes Surriage.
—— Begum's Daughter.
Cable (G. W.) Bonaventure, 5*s.*
Coleridge (C. R.) English Squire.
Craddock, Despot of Broomsedge.
Croker (Mrs. B. M.) Some One Else.
Cumberland (Stuart) Vasty Deep.
De Leon, Under the Stars and Crescent.
Edwards (Miss Betham) Half-way.
Eggleston, Juggernaut.
French Heiress in her own Chateau.
Gilliat (E.) Story of the Dragonnades.
Hardy (A. S.) Passe-rose.
—— (Thos.) Far from the Madding.
—— Hand of Ethelberta.
—— Laodicean.
—— Mayor of Casterbridge.
—— Pair of Blue Eyes.
—— Return of the Native.
—— Trumpet-Major.
—— Two on a Tower.
Harkut, Conspirator.
Hatton (J.) Old House at Sandwich.
—— Three Recruits.
Hoey (Mrs. Cashel) Golden Sorrow.
—— Out of Court.
—— Stern Chase.
Howard (Blanche W.) Open Door.
Ingelow (Jean) Don John.
—— John Jerome, 5*s.*
—— Sarah de Berenger.
Lathrop, Newport, 5*s.*
Mac Donald (Geo.) Adela Cathcart.
—— Guild Court.

Low's Stand. Novels—continued.
Mac Donald (Geo.) Mary Marston.
—— Orts.
—— Stephen Archer, &c.
—— The Vicar's Daughter.
—— Weighed and Wanting.
Macmaster, Our Pleasant Vices.
Macquoid (Mrs.) Diane.
Musgrave (Mrs.) Miriam.
Osborn, Spell of Ashtaroth, 5s.
Prince Maskiloff.
Riddell (Mrs.) Alaric Spenceley.
—— Daisies and Buttercups.
—— Senior Partner.
—— Struggle for Fame.
Russell (W. Clark) Betwixt the Forelands.
—— Frozen Pirate.
—— Jack's Courtship.
—— John Holdsworth.
—— Little Loo.
—— My Watch Below.
—— Ocean Free Lance.
—— Sailor's Sweetheart.
—— Sea Queen.
—— Strange Voyage.
—— The Lady Maud.
—— Wreck of the *Grosvenor*.
Steuart, Kilgroom.
Stockton (F. R.) Ardis Claverden.
—— Bee-man of Orn, 5s.
—— Hundredth Man.
—— The late Mrs. Null.
Stoker, Snake's Pass.
Stowe (Mrs.) Old Town Folk.
—— Poganuc People.
Thomas, House on the Scar.
Thomson, Ulu, an African Romance.
Tourgee, Murvale Eastman.
Tytler (S.) Duchess Frances.
Vane, From the Dead.
Wallace (Lew.) Ben Hur.
Warner, Little Journey in the World.
Woolson (Constance Fenimore) Anne.
—— East Angles.
—— For the Major, 5s.
—— Jupiter Lights.

See also Sea Stories.

Low's Stand. Novels, new issue at short intervals, 2s. 6d. and 2s.
Blackmore, Alice Lorraine.
—— Christowell.
—— Clara Vaughan.
—— Cripps the Carrier.
—— Kit and Kitty.
—— Lorna Doone.
—— Mary Anerley.
—— Tommy Upmore.
Cable, Bonaventure.
Croker, Some One Else.
Cumberland, Vasty Deep.
De Leon, Under the Stars.
Edwards, Half-way.
Hardy, Laodicean.
—— Madding Crowd.
—— Mayor of Casterbridge.
—— Trumpet-Major,
—— Two on a Tower.
Hatton, Old House at Sandwich.
—— Three Recruits.
Hoey, Golden Sorrow.
—— Out of Court.
—— Stern Chase.
Holmes, Guardian Angel.
Ingelow, John Jerome.
—— Sarah de Berenger.
Mac Donald, Adela Cathcart.
—— Guild Court.
—— Stephen Archer.
—— Vicar's Daughter.
Oliphant, Innocent.
Riddell, Daisies and Buttercups.
—— Senior Partner.
Stockton, Bee-man of Orn, 5s.
—— Dusantes.
—— Mrs. Lecks and Mrs. Aleshine.
Stowe, Dred.
—— Old Town Folk.
—— Poganuc People.
Thomson, Ulu.
Walford, Her Great Idea, &c., Stories.
Low's German Series, a graduated course. See "German."
Low's Readers. See English Reader and French Reader.
Low's Standard Books for Boys, with numerous illustrations, 2s. 6d. each; gilt edges, 3s. 6d.

Low's Stand. Books for Boys—continued.

Adventures in New Guinea: the Narrative of Louis Tregance.
Biart (Lucien) Adventures of a Young Naturalist.
—— My Rambles in the New World.
Boussenard, Crusoes of Guiana.
—— Gold Seekers, a sequel to the above.
Butler (Col. Sir Wm., K.C.B.) Red Cloud, the Solitary Sioux: a Tale of the Great Prairie.
Cahun (Leon) Adventures of Captain Mago.
—— Blue Banner.
Célière, Startling Exploits of the Doctor.
Chaillu (Paul du) Wild Life under the Equator.
Collingwood (Harry) Under the Meteor Flag.
—— Voyage of the *Aurora*.
Cozzens (S.W.) Marvellous Country.
Dodge (Mrs.) Hans Brinker; or, The Silver Skates.
Du Chaillu (Paul) Stories of the Gorilla Country.
Erckmann - Chatrian, Brothers Rantzau.
Fenn (G.Manville) Off to the Wilds.
—— Silver Cañon.
Groves (Percy) Charmouth Grange; a Tale of the 17th Century.
Heldmann (B.) Mutiny on Board the Ship *Leander*.
Henty (G. A.) Cornet of Horse: a Tale of Marlborough's Wars.
—— Jack Archer; a Tale of the Crimea.
—— Winning his Spurs: a Tale of the Crusades.
Johnstone (D. Lawson) Mountain Kingdom.
Kennedy (E. B.) Blacks and Bushrangers in Queensland.
Kingston (W. H. G.) Ben Burton; or, Born and Bred at Sea.
—— Captain Mugford; or, Our Salt and Fresh Water Tutors.
—— Dick Cheveley.
—— Heir of Kilfinnan.

Low's Stand. Books for Boys—continued.

Kingston (W. H. G.) Snowshoes and Canoes.
—— Two Supercargoes.
—— With Axe and Rifle on the Western Prairies.
Laurie (A.) Conquest of the Moon.
—— New York to Brest in Seven Hours.
MacGregor (John) A Thousand Miles in the *Rob Roy* Canoe on Rivers and Lakes of Europe.
Maclean (H. E.) Maid of the Ship *Golden Age*.
Meunier, Great Hunting Grounds of the World.
Muller, Noble Words and Deeds.
Perelaer, The Three Deserters; or, Ran Away from the Dutch.
Reed (Talbot Baines) Sir Ludar: a Tale of the Days of the Good Queen Bess.
Rousselet (Louis) Drummer-boy: a Story of the Time of Washington.
—— King of the Tigers.
—— Serpent Charmer.
—— Son of the Constable of France.
Russell (W. Clark) Frozen Pirates.
Stanley, My Kalulu—Prince, King and Slave.
Winder (F. H.) Lost in Africa.

Low's Standard Series of Books by popular writers, cloth gilt, 2s.; gilt edges, 2s. 6d. each.

Alcott (L. M.) A Rose in Bloom.
—— An Old-Fashioned Girl.
—— Aunt Jo's Scrap Bag.
—— Eight Cousins, illust.
—— Jack and Jill.
—— Jimmy's Cruise.
—— Little Men.
—— Little Women and Little Women Wedded.
—— Lulu's Library, illust.
—— Shawl Straps.
—— Silver Pitchers.
—— Spinning-Wheel Stories.
—— Under the Lilacs, illust.
—— Work and Beginning Again, Ill.

Low's Stand. Series—continued.
Alden (W. L.) Jimmy Brown, illust.
—— Trying to Find Europe.
Bunyan (John) Pilgrim's Progress, (extra volume), gilt, 2s.
De Witt (Madame) An Only Sister.
Francis (Francis) Eric and Ethel, illust.
Holm (Saxe) Draxy Miller's Dowry.
Jerdon (Gert.) Keyhole Country, illust.
Robinson (Phil) In My Indian Garden.
—— Under the Punkah.
Roe (E. P.) Nature's Serial Story.
Saintine, Picciola.
Samuels, Forecastle to Cabin, illust.
Sandeau (Jules) Seagull Rock.
Stowe (Mrs.) Dred.
—— Ghost in the Mill, &c.
—— My Wife and I.
—— We and our Neighbours.
See also Low's Standard Series.
Tooley (Mrs.) Life of Harriet Beecher Stowe.
Warner (C. Dudley) In the Wilderness.
—— My Summer in a Garden.
Whitney (Mrs.) A Summer in Leslie Goldthwaite's Life.
—— Faith Gartney's Girlhood.
—— Hitherto.
—— Real Folks.
—— The Gayworthys.
—— We Girls.
—— The Other Girls : a Sequel.
⁎⁎ *A new illustrated list of books for boys and girls, with portraits of celebrated authors, sent post free on application.*

LOWELL, J. R., *Among my Books*, Series I. and II., 7s. 6d. each.
—— *My Study Windows*, n. ed. 1s.
—— *Vision of Sir Launfal*, illus. 63s.

MACDONALD, A., *Our Sceptred Isle*, 3s. 6d.
—— D., *Oceania*, 6s.

MACDONALD, Geo., *Castle Warlock, a Homely Romance*, 3 vols. 31s. 6d.
—— See also Low's Standard Novels.
—— Sir John A., *Life.*

MACDOWALL, Alex. B., *Curve Pictures of London*, 1s.

MACGAHAN, J. A., *Oxus*, 7s. 6d.

MACGOUN, *Commercial Correspondence*, 5s.

MACGREGOR, J., *Rob Roy in the Baltic*, n. ed. 3s. 6d. and 2s. 6d.
——. *Rob Roy Canoe*, new edit., 3s. 6d. and 2s. 6d.
—— *Yawl Rob Roy*, new edit., 3s. 6d. and 2s. 6d.

MACKENNA, *Brave Men in Action*, 10s. 6d.

MACKENZIE, Sir Morell, *Fatal Illness of Frederick the Noble*, 2s. 6d.

MACKINNON and SHADBOLT, *South African Campaign*, 50s.

MACLAREN, A. See Preachers.

MACLEAN, H. E. See Low's Standard Books.

MACMASTER. See Low's Standard Novels.

MACMURDO, E., *History of Portugal*, 21s.; II. 21s.; III. 21s.

MAHAN, A. T., *Influence of Sea Power on History*, 18s.

Maid of Florence, 10s. 6d.

MAIN, Mrs., *High Life*, 10s. 6d.
—— See also Burnaby, Mrs.

MALAN, A. N., *Cobbler of Cornikeranium*, 5s.
—— C. F. de M., *Eric and Connie's Cruise*, 5s.

Man's Thoughts. See Gentle Life Series.

MANLEY, J. J., *Fish and Fishing*, 6s.

MANTEGNA and FRANCIA.
See Great Artists.

MARCH, F. A., *Comparative Anglo-Saxon Grammar*, 12s.

—— *Anglo-Saxon Reader*, 7s. 6d.

MARKHAM, ADM., *Naval Career*, 14s.

—— *Whaling Cruise*, new edit. 7s. 6d.

—— C. R., *Peru*. See Foreign Countries.

—— *Fighting Veres*, 18s.

—— *War Between Peru and Chili*, 10s. 6d.

MARSH, G. P., *Lectures on the English Language*, 18s.

—— *Origin and History of the English Language*, 18s.

MARSHALL, W. G., *Through America*, new edit. 7s. 6d.

MARSTON, E., *How Stanley wrote " In Darkest Africa,"* 1s.

—— See also Amateur Angler, Frank's Ranche, and Fresh Woods.

—— W., *Eminent Actors*, n. ed. 6s.

MARTIN, J. W., *Float Fishing and Spinning*, new edit. 2s.

Massage. See Nursing Record Series.

MATTHEWS, J. W., *Incwadi Yami*, 14s.

MAURY, M. F., *Life*, 12s. 6d.

—— *Physical Geography and Meteorology of the Sea*, new ed. 6s.

MEISSNER, A. L., *Children's Own German Book* (Low's Series), 1s. 6d.

—— *First German Reader* (Low's Series), 1s. 6d.

—— *Second German Reader* (Low's Series), 1s. 6d.

MEISSONIER. See Great Artists.

MELBOURNE, LORD. See Prime Ministers.

MELIO, G. L., *Swedish Drill*, 1s. 6d.

MENDELSSOHN *Family*, 1729-1847, Letters and Journals, 2 vols. 30s.; new edit. 30s.

—— See also Great Musicians.

MERRIFIELD, J., *Nautical Astronomy*, 7s. 6d.

MERRYLEES, J., *Carlsbad*, 7s. 6d. and 9s.

MESNEY,W., *Tungking*,3s. 6d.

Metal Workers' Recipes and Processes, by W. T. Brannt, 12s.6d.

MEUNIER, V. See Low's Standard Books.

Michelangelo. See Great Artists.

MILFORD, P. *Ned Stafford's Experiences*, 5s.

MILL, JAMES. See English Philosophers.

MILLS, J., *Alternative Elementary Chemistry*, 1s. 6d.

—— *Chemistry Based on the Science and Art Syllabus*, 2s. 6d.

—— *Elementary Chemistry*, answers, 2 vols. 1s. each.

MILTON'S *Allegro.* See Choice Editions.

MITCHELL, D.G.(Ik. Marvel) *English Lands, Letters and Kings*, 2 vols. 6s. each.

—— *Writings*, new edit. per vol. 5s.

MITFORD, J., *Letters*, 3s. 6d.

—— MISS, *Our Village*, illust. 5s.

Modern Etchings, 63s. & 31s.6d.

MOLLETT, J. W., *Dictionary of Words in Art and Archæology*, illust. 15s.

—— *Etched Examples*, 31s. 6d. and 63s.

—— See also Great Artists.

MONCK. See English Philosophers.

MONEY, E., *The Truth About America*, 6s.; new edit. 2s. 6d.

MONKHOUSE. See G. Artists.

Montaigne's Essays, revised by J. Hain Friswell, 2s. 6d.

—— See Gentle Life Series.

MOORE, J. M., *New Zealand for Emigrant, Invalid, and Tourist*, 5s.

MORFILL, W. R., *Russia*, 3s. 6d.

MORLEY, HENRY, *English Literature in the Reign of Victoria*, 2s. 6d.

—— *Five Centuries of English Literature*, 2s.

MORSE, E. S., *Japanese Homes*, new edit. 10s. 6d.

MORTEN, *Hospital Life*, 1s.

MORTIMER, J., *Chess Player's Pocket-Book*, new edit. 1s.

MORWOOD, V.S., *Our Gipsies*, 18s.

MOSS, F. J., *Great South Sea*, 8s. 6d.

MOSSMAN, S., *Japan*, 3s. 6d.

MOTTI, PIETRO, *Elementary Russian Grammar*, 2s. 6d.

—— *Russian Conversation Grammar*, 5s.; Key, 2s.

MOULE, H. C. G., *Sermons*, 3s. 6d.

MOXLEY, *West India Sanatorium, and Barbados*, 3s. 6d.

MOXON, W., *Pilocereus Senilis*, 3s. 6d.

MOZART, 3s. Gr. Musicians.

MULLER, E. See Low's Standard Books.

MULLIN, J.P., *Moulding and Pattern Making*, 12s. 6d.

MULREADY, 3s. 6d. Great Artists.

MURILLO. See Great Artists.

MUSGRAVE, MRS. See Low's Standard Novels.

—— *SavageLondon*, n. e. 3s. 6d.

My Comforter, &c., Religious Poems, 2s. 6d.

Napoleon I. See Bayard Series.

Napoleon I. and Marie Louise, 7s. 6d.

NELSON, WOLFRED, *Panama*, 6s.

Nelson's Words and Deeds, 3s. 6d.

NETHERCOTE, *Pytchley Hunt*, 8s. 6d.

New Democracy, 1s.

New Zealand, chromos, by Barraud, 168s.

NICHOLSON, *British Association Work and Workers*, 1s.

Nineteenth Century, a Monthly Review, 2s. 6d. per No.

NISBET, HUME, *Life and Nature Studies*, 6s.

NIXON, *Story of the Transvaal*, 12s. 6d.

Nordenskiöld's Voyage, trans. 21s.

NORDHOFF, C., *California*, new edit. 12s. 6d.

NORRIS, RACHEL, *Nursing Notes*, 2s.

NORTH, W., *Roman Fever*, 25s.

Northern Fairy Tales, 5s

NORTON, C. L., *Florida*, 5s.

NORWAY, G., *How Martin Drake Found his Father* illus. 5s.

NUGENT'S *French Dictionary*, new edit. 3s.

Nuggets of the Gouph, 3s.

Nursing Record Series, text books and manuals. Edited by Charles. F. Rideal.

1. Lectures to Nurses on Antiseptics in Surgery. By E. Stanmore Bishop. With coloured plates, 2s.

Nursing Record Series—contin.

2. **Nursing Notes.** Medical and Surgical information. For Hospital Nurses, &c. With illustrations and a glossary of terms. By Rachel Norris (*née* Williams), late Acting Superintendent of Royal Victoria Military Hospital at Suez, 2*s.*

3. **Practical Electro-Therapeutics.** By Arthur Harries, M.D., and H. Newman Lawrence. With photographs and diagrams, 1*s.*6*d.*

4. **Massage for Beginners.** Simple and easy directions for learning and remembering the different movements. By Lucy Fitch, 1*s.*

O'BRIEN, *Fifty Years of Concession to Ireland*, vol. i. 16*s.*; vol. ii. 16*s.*

—— *Irish Land Question*, 2*s.*

OGDEN, JAMES, *Fly - tying*, 2*s.* 6*d.*

O'GRADY, *Bardic Literature of Ireland*, 1*s.*

—— *History of Ireland*, vol. i. 7*s.* 6*d.*; ii. 7*s.* 6*d.*

Old Masters in Photo. 73*s.* 6*d.*

Orient Line Guide, new edit. 2*s.* 6*d.*

ORLEBAR, *Sancta Christina*, 5*s.*

Other People's Windows. See Gentle Life Series.

OTTÉ, *Denmark and Iceland*, 3*s.* 6*d.* Foreign Countries.

Our Little Ones in Heaven, 5*s.*

Out of School at Eton, 2*s.* 6*d.*

OVERBECK. See Great Artists.

OWEN, DOUGLAS, *Marine Insurance*, 15*s.*

Oxford Days, by a M.A., 2*s.* 6*d.*

PALGRAVE, *Chairman's Handbook*, new edit. 2*s.*

—— *Oliver Cromwell*, 10*s.* 6*d.*

PALLISER, *China Collector's Companion*, 5*s.*

—— *History of Lace*, n. ed. 21*s.*

PANTON, *Homes of Taste*, 2*s.*6*d.*

PARKE, *Emin Pasha Relief Expedition*, 21*s.*

PARKER, E. H., *Chinese Account of the Opium War*, 1*s.* 6*d.*

PARSONS, J., *Principles of Partnership*, 31*s.* 6*d.*

—— T. P., *Marine Insurance*, 2 vols. 63*s.*

PEACH, *Annals of Swainswick*, 10*s.* 6*d.*

Peel. See Prime Ministers.

PELLESCHI, G., *Gran Chaco*, 8*s.* 6*d.*

PENNELL, H. C., *Fishing Tackle*, 2*s.*

—— *Sporting Fish*, 15*s.* & 30*s.*

Penny Postage Jubilee, 1*s.*

PERRY, NORA, *Another Flock of Girls*, illus. by Birch & Copeland, 7*s.* 6*d.*

Peru, 3*s.* 6*d.* Foreign Countries.

PHELPS, E. S., *Struggle for Immortality*, 5*s.*

—— SAMUEL, *Life*, by W. M. Phelps and Forbes-Robertson, 12*s.*

PHILLIMORE, C. M., *Italian Literature*, new. edit. 3*s.* 6*d.*

PHILLIPPS, W. M., *English Elegies*, 5*s.*

PHILLIPS, L. P., *Dictionary of Biographical Reference*, new. edit. 25*s.*

—— W., *Law of Insurance*, 2 vols. 73*s.* 6*d.*

PHILPOT, H. J., *Diabetes Mellitus*, 5*s.*

—— *Diet Tables*, 1*s.* each.

Picture Gallery of British Art. I. to VI. 18*s.* each.

—— *Modern Art*, 3 vols. 31*s.*6*d.* each.

PINTO, *How I Crossed Africa*, 2 vols. 42*s.*

Playtime Library. See Humphrey and Huntingdon.

Pleasant History of Reynard the Fox, trans. by T. Roscoe, illus. 7*s.* 6*d.*

POCOCK, R., *Gravesend Historian*, 5*s.*

POE, by E. C. Stedman, 3*s.* 6*d.*

—— *Raven*, ill. by G. Doré, 63*s.*

Poems of the Inner Life, 5*s.*

Poetry of Nature. See Choice Editions.

Poetry of the Anti-Jacobin, 7*s.* 6*d.* and 21*s.*

POOLE, *Somerset Customs and Legends*, 5*s.*

—— S. LANE, *Egypt*, 3*s.* 6*d.* Foreign Countries.

POPE, *Select Poetical Works*, (Bernhard Tauchnitz Collection), 2*s.*

PORCHER, A., *Juvenile* French Plays, 1*s.*

Portraits of Racehorses, 4 vols. 126*s.*

POSSELT, *Structure of Fibres*, 63*s.*

—— *Textile Design*, illust. 28*s.*

POYNTER. See Illustrated Text Books.

Preachers of the Age, 3*s.* 6*d.* ea. Living Theology, by His Grace the Archbishop of Canterbury. The Conquering Christ, by Rev. A. Maclaren. *Verbum Crucis*, by the Bishop of Derry. Ethical Christianity, by H. P. Hughes. Sermons, by Canon W. J. Knox-Little. Light and Peace, by H. R. Reynolds. Faith and Duty, by A. M. Fairbairn. Plain Words on Great Themes, by J. O. Dykes. Sermons, by the Bishop of Ripon.

Preachers of the Age—continued. Sermons, by Rev. C. H. Spurgeon. *Agonia Christi*, by Dean Lefroy, of Norwich. Sermons, by H. C. G. Moule, M.A. *Volumes will follow in quick succession by other well-known men.*

Prime Ministers, a series of political biographies, edited by Stuart J. Reid, 3*s.* 6*d.* each.
1. Earl of Beaconsfield, by J. Anthony Froude.
2. Viscount Melbourne, by Henry Dunckley ("*Verax*").
3. Sir Robert Peel, by Justin McCarthy.
4. Viscount Palmerston, by the Marquis of Lorne.
5. Earl Russell, by Stuart J. Reid.
6. Right Hon. W. E. Gladstone, by G. W. E. Russell.
7. Earl of Aberdeen, by Sir Arthur Gordon.
8. Marquis of Salisbury, by H. D. Traill.
9. Earl of Derby, by George Saintsbury.
₊ *An edition, limited to 250 copies, is issued on hand-made paper, medium 8vo, bound in half vellum, cloth sides, gilt top. Price for the 9 vols. 4l. 4s. nett.*

Prince Maskiloff. See Low's Standard Novels.

Prince of Nursery Playmates, new edit. 2*s.* 6*d.*

PRITT, T. N., *Country Trout Flies*, 10*s.* 6*d.*

Reynolds. See Great Artists.

Purcell. See Great Musicians.

QUILTER, H., *Giotto, Life*, &c. 15*s.*

RAMBAUD, *History of Russia*, new edit., 3 vols. 21*s.*

RAPHAEL. See Great Artists.

REDFORD, *Sculpture.* See Illustrated Text-books.

REDGRAVE, *Engl. Painters*, 10*s.* 6*d.* and 12*s.*

REED, Sir E. J., *Modern Ships of War*, 10s. 6d.
—— T. B., *Roger Ingleton, Minor*, 5s.
—— *Sir Ludar.* See Low's Standard Books.
REID, Mayne, Capt., *Stories of Strange Adventures*, illust. 5s.
—— Stuart J. See Prime Ministers.
—— T. Wemyss, *Land of the Bey*, 10s. 6d.
Remarkable Bindings in British Museum, 168s.; 94s. 6d.; 73s. 6d. and 63s.
REMBRANDT. See Great Artists.
Reminiscences of a Boyhood, 6s.
REMUSAT, *Memoirs*, Vols. I. and II. new ed. 16s. each.
—— *Select Letters*, 16s.
REYNOLDS. See Gr. Artists.
—— Henry R., *Light & Peace, &c. Sermons*, 3s. 6d.
RICHARDS, J. W., *Aluminium*, new edit. 21s.
RICHARDSON, *Choice of Books*, 3s. 6d.
RICHTER, J. P., *Italian Art*, 42s.
—— See also Great Artists.
RIDDELL. See Low's Standard Novels.
RIDEAL, *Women of the Time*, 14s.
RIFFAULT, *Colours for Painting*, 31s. 6d.
RIIS, *How the Other Half Lives*, 10s. 6d.
RIPON, Bp. of. See Preachers.
ROBERTS, Miss, *France.* See Foreign Countries.
—— W., *English Bookselling*, earlier history, 7s. 6d.
ROBIDA, A., *Toilette*, coloured, 7s. 6d.

ROBINSON, "*Romeo*" *Coates*, 7s. 6d.
—— *Noah's Ark*, n. ed. 3s. 6d.
—— *Sinners & Saints*, 10s. 6d.
—— See also Low's Standard Series.
—— *Wealth and its Sources*, 5s.
—— W. C., *Law of Patents*, 3 vols. 105s.
ROCHEFOUCAULD. See Bayard Series.
ROCKSTRO, *History of Music*, new ed. 14s.
RODRIGUES, *Panama Canal*, 5s.
ROE, E. P. See Low's Standard Series.
ROGERS, S. See Choice Editions.
ROLFE, *Pompeii*, 7s. 6d.
Romantic Stories of the Legal Profession, 7s. 6d.
ROMNEY. See Great Artists.
ROOSEVELT, Blanche R. *Home Life of Longfellow*, 7s. 6d.
ROSE, J., *Mechanical Drawing*, 16s.
—— *Practical Machinist*, new ed. 12s. 6d.
—— *Key to Engines*, 8s. 6d.
—— *Modern Steam Engines*, 31s. 6d.
—— *Steam Boilers*, 12s. 6d.
Rose Library. Popular Literature of all countries, per vol. 1s., unless the price is given.
Alcott (L. M.) *Eight Cousins*, 2s.; cloth, 3s. 6d.
—— *Jack and Jill*, 2s.; cloth, 5s.
—— *Jimmy's cruise in the Pinafore*, 2s.; cloth, 3s. 6d.
—— *Little Women.*
—— *Little Women Wedded;* Nos. 4 and 5 in 1 vol. cloth, 3s. 6d.
—— *Little Men*, 2s.; cloth gilt, 3s. 6d.

Rose Library—continued.
Alcott (L. M.) Old-fashioned Girls, 2*s.*; cloth, 3*s.* 6*d.*
—— Rose in Bloom, 2*s.*; cl. 3*s.* 6*d.*
—— Silver Pitchers.
—— Under the Lilacs, 2*s.*; cloth, 3*s.* 6*d.*
—— Work, A Story of Experience, 2 vols. in 1, cloth, 3*s.* 6*d.*
Stowe (Mrs.) Pearl of Orr's Island.
—— Minister's Wooing.
—— We and Our Neighbours, 2*s.*
—— My Wife and I, 2*s.*
Dodge (Mrs.) Hans Brinker, or, The Silver Skates, 1*s.*; cloth, 5*s.*; 3*s.* 6*d.*; 2*s.* 6*t.*
Lowell (J. R.) My Study Windows.
Holmes (Oliver Wendell) Guardian Angel, cloth, 2*s.*
Warner (C. D.) My Summer in a Garden, cloth, 2*s.*
Stowe (Mrs.) Dred, 2*s.*; cloth gilt, 3*s.* 6*d.*
Carleton (W.) City Ballads, 2 vols. in 1, cloth gilt, 2*s.* 6*d.*
—— Legends, 2 vols. in 1, cloth gilt, 2*s.* 6*d.*
—— Farm Ballads, 6*d.* and 9*d.*; 3 vols. in 1, cloth gilt, 3*s.* 6*d.*
—— Farm Festivals, 3 vols. in 1, cloth gilt, 3*s.* 6*d.*
—— Farm Legends, 3 vols. in 1, cloth gilt, 3*s.* 6*d.*
Clients of Dr. Bernagius, 2 vols.
Howells (W. D.) Undiscovered Country.
Clay (C. M.) Baby Rue.
—— Story of Helen Troy.
Whitney (Mrs.) Hitherto, 2 vols. cloth, 3*s.* 6*d.*
Fawcett (E.) Gentleman of Leisure.
Butler, Nothing to Wear.
ROSS, MARS, *Cantabria*, 21*s.*
ROSSINI, &c., See Great Musicians.
Rothschilds, by J. Reeves, 7*s.* 6*d.*
Roughing it after Gold, by Rux, new edit. 1*s.*
ROUSSELET.   See Low's Standard Books.

ROWBOTHAM, F. J., *Prairie Land*, 5*s.*
Royal Naval Exhibition, a souvenir, illus. 1*s.*
RUBENS.   See Great Artists.
RUGGLES, H. J., *Shakespeare's Method*, 7*s.* 6*d.*
RUSSELL, G.W.E., *Gladstone.* See Prime Ministers.
—— W. CLARK, *Mrs. Dines' Jewels*, 2*s.* 6*d.*
—— *Nelson's. Words and Deeds*, 3*s.* 6*d.*
—— *Sailor's Language*, illus. 3*s.* 6*d.*
—— See also Low's Standard Novels and Sea Stories.
—— W. HOWARD, *Prince of Wales' Tour*, illust. 52*s.* 6*d.* and 84*s.*
Russia.   See Foreign Countries.
Saints and their Symbols, 3*s.* 6*d.*
SAINTSBURY, G., *Earl of Derby.* See Prime Ministers.
SAINTINE, *Picciola*, 2*s.* 6*d.* and 2*s.* See Low's Standard Series.
SALISBURY, LORD. See Prime Ministers.
SAMUELS.   See Low's Standard Series.
SANDARS, *German Primer*, 1*s.*
SANDEAU, *Seagull Rock*, 2*s.* and 2*s.* 6*d.* Low's Standard Series.
SANDLANDS, *How to Develop Vocal Power*, 1*s.*
SAUER, *European Commerce*, 5*s.*
—— *Italian Grammar* (Key, 2*s.*), 5*s.*
—— *Spanish Dialogues*, 2*s.* 6*d.*
—— *Spanish Grammar* (Key, 2*s.*), 5*s.*
—— *Spanish Reader*, new edit. 3*s.* 6*d.*
SAUNDERS, J., *Jaspar Deane*, 10*s.* 6*d.*

SCHAACK, M. J., *Anarchy*, 16*s*.

SCHAUERMANN, *Ornament for technical schools*, 10*s*. 6*d*.

SCHERER, *Essays in English Literature*, by G. Saintsbury, 6*s*.

SCHERR, *English Literature*, history, 8*s*. 6*d*.

SCHILLER'S *Prosa*, selections by Buchheim. Low's Series 2*s*. 6*d*.

SCHUBERT. See Great Musicians.

SCHUMANN. See Great Musicians.

SCHWEINFURTH. See Low's Standard Library.

Scientific Education of Dogs, 6*s*.

SCOTT, Leader, *Renaissance of Art in Italy*, 31*s*. 6*d*.

—— See also Illust. Text-books.

—— Sir Gilbert, *Autobiography*, 18*s*.

—— W. B. See Great Artists.

SELMA, Robert, *Poems*, 5*s*.

SERGEANT, L. See Foreign Countries.

Shadow of the Rock, 2*s*. 6*d*.

SHAFTESBURY. See English Philosophers.

SHAKESPEARE, ed. by R. G. White, 3 vols. 36*s*.; *édit. de luxe*, 63*s*.

—— *Annals; Life & Work*, 2*s*.

—— *Hamlet*, 1603, also 1604, 7*s*. 6*d*.

—— *Hamlet*, by Karl Elze, 12*s*. 6*d*.

—— *Heroines*, by living painters, 105*s*.; artists' proofs, 630*s*.

—— *Macbeth*, with etchings, 105*s*. and 52*s*. 6*d*.

—— *Songs and Sonnets*. See Choice Editions.

—— *Taming of the Shrew*, adapted for drawing-room, paper wrapper, 1*s*.

SHEPHERD, *British School of Painting*, 2nd edit. 6*s*.; 3rd edit. sewed, 1*s*.

SHERIDAN, *Rivals*, col. plates, 52*s*. 6*d*. nett; art. pr. 105*s*. nett.

SHIELDS, G. O., *Big Game of North America*, 21*s*.

—— *Cruisings in the Cascades*, 10*s*. 6*d*.

SHOCK, W. H., *Steam Boilers*, 73*s*. 6*d*.

SIDNEY. See Gentle Life Series.

Silent Hour. See Gentle Life Series.

SIMKIN, *Our Armies*, plates in imitation of water-colour (5 parts at 1*s*.), 6*s*.

SIMSON, *Ecuador and the Putumayor*, 8*s*. 6*d*.

SKOTTOWE, *Hanoverian Kings*, new edit. 8*s*. 6*d*.

SLOANE, T. O., *Home Experiments*, 6*s*.

SMITH, HAMILTON, and LEGROS' *French Dictionary*, 2 vols. 16*s*., 21*s*., and 22*s*.

SMITH, Edward, *Cobbett*, 2 vols. 24*s*.

—— G., *Assyria*, 18*s*.

—— *Chaldean Account of Genesis*, new edit. by Sayce, 18*s*.

—— Gerard. See Illustrated Text Books.

—— T. Roger. See Illustrated Text Books.

Socrates. See Bayard Series.

SOMERSET, *Our Village Life*, 5*s*.

Spain. See Foreign Countries.

SPAYTH, *Draught Player*, new edit. 12*s*. 6*d*.

SPIERS, *French Dictionary*, 2 vols. 18*s*., half bound, 2 vols., 21*s*.

SPRY. See Low's Stand. Library.

SPURGEON, C. H. See
Preachers.

STANLEY, H. M., *Congo*, 2
vols. 42s. and 21s.

—— *In Darkest Africa*, 2 vols.,
42s.

—— *Emin's Rescue*, 1s.

—— See also Low's Standard
Library and Low's Standard
Books.

START, *Exercises in Mensuration*, 8d.

STEPHENS, F. G., *Celebrated
Flemish and French Pictures*,
with notes, 28s.

—— See also Great Artists.

STERNE. See Bayard Series.

STERRY, J. ASHBY, *Cucumber
Chronicles*, 5s.

STEUART, J. A., *Letters to
Living Authors*, new edit. 2s. 6d.;
édit. de luxe, 10s. 6d.

—— See also Low's Standard
Novels.

STEVENS, J. W., *Practical
Workings of the Leather Manufacture*, illust. 18s.

—— T., *Around the World on
a Bicycle*, over 100 illust. 16s.;
part II. 16s.

STEWART, DUGALD, *Outlines
of Moral Philosophy*, 3s. 6d.

STOCKTON, F. R., *Casting
Away of Mrs. Lecks*, 1s.

—— *The Dusantes*, a sequel, 1s.

—— *Merry Chanter*, 2s. 6d.

—— *Personally Conducted*,
illust. by Joseph Pennell, 7s. 6d.

—— *Rudder Grangers Abroad*,
2s. 6d.

—— *Squirrel Inn*, illust. 6s.

—— *Story of Viteau*, illust. 5s.
new edit. 3s. 6d.

—— *Three Burglars*, 1s. & 2s.

—— See also Low's Standard
Novels.

STORER, F. H., *Agriculture*,
2 vols., 25s.

STOWE, EDWIN. See Great
Artists.

—— MRS., *Flowers and Fruit
from Her Writings*, 3s. 6d.

—— *Life . . . her own Words*
. . . *Letters and Original Composition*, 15s.

—— *Life*, told for boys and
girls, by S. A. Tooley, 5s., new
edit. 2s. 6d. and 2s.

—— *Little Foxes*, cheap edit.
1s.; 4s. 6d.

—— *Minister's Wooing*, 1s.

—— *Pearl of Orr's Island*,
3s. 6d. and 1s.

—— *Uncle Tom's Cabin*, with
126 new illust. 2 vols. 18s.

—— See also Low's Standard
Novels and Low's Standard Series.

STRACHAN, J., *New Guinea*,
12s.

STRANAHAN, *French Painting*, 21s.

STRICKLAND, F., *Engadine*,
new edit. 5s.

STUTFIELD, El Maghreb,
ride through Morocco, 8s. 6d.

SUMNER, C., *Memoir*, new
edit. 2 vols. 36s.

Sweden and Norway. See
Foreign Countries.

Sylvanus Redivivus, 10s. 6d.

SZCZEPANSKI, Technical
Literature, a directory, 2s.

TAINE, H. A., *Origines*,
I. Ancient Régime, French Revolution, 3 vols.; Modern Régime,
vol. I. 16s.

TAYLOR, H., *English Constitution*, 18s.

—— R. L., *Analysis Tables*, 1s.

—— *Chemistry*, 1s. 6d.

Techno-Chemical Receipt Book,
10s. 6d.

TENNYSON. See Choice Editions.
Ten Years of a Sailor's Life, 7s. 6d.
THAUSING, *Malt and Beer,* 45s.
THEAKSTON,*British Angling Flies,* 5s.
Thomas à Kempis Birthday-Book, 3s. 6d.
—— *Daily Text-Book,* 2s. 6d.
—— See also Gentle Life Series.
THOMAS, BERTHA, *House on the Scar, Tale of South Devon,* 6s.
THOMSON, JOSEPH. See Low's Standard Library and Low's Standard Novels.
—— W., *Algebra,* 5s.; without Answers, 4s. 6d.; Key, 1s. 6d.
THORNTON, W. · PUGIN, *Heads, and what they tell us,* 1s.
THORODSEN, J. P., *Lad and Lass,* 6s.
TICKNOR, G., *Memoir,* new edit., 2 vols. 21s.
TILESTON, MARY W., *Daily Strength,* 4s. 6t.
TINTORETTO. See Great Artists.
TITIAN. See Great Artists.
TODD, *Life,* by J. E. Todd, 12s.
TOURGEE. See Low's Standard Novels.
TOY, C. H., *Judaism,* 14s.
Tracks in Norway, 2s., n. ed. 1s.
TRAILL. See Prime Ministers.
Transactions of the Hong Kong Medical Society, vol. I. 12s. 6d.
TROMHOLT, *Aurora Borealis,* 2 vols., 30s.
TUCKER, *Eastern Europe,* 15s.
TUCKERMAN, B., *English Fiction,* 8s. 6d.
—— *Lafayette,* 2 vols. 12s.
TURNER, J. M. W. See Gr. Artists.

TYSON, *Arctic Adventures,* 25s.
TYTLER, SARAH. See Low's Standard Novels.
—— M. C., *American Literature,* vols. I. and II. 24s.
UPTON, H., *Dairy Farming,* 2s.
Valley Council, by P. Clarke, 6s.
VANDYCK and HALS. See Great Artists.
VANE, DENZIL, *Lynn's Court Mystery,* 1s.
—— See also Low's Standard Novels.
Vane, Young Sir Harry, 18s.
VELAZQUEZ. See Gr. Artists.
—— and MURILLO, by C. B. Curtis, with etchings, 31s. 6d. and 63s.
VERE, SIR F., *Fighting Veres,* 18s.
VERNE, J., *Works by.* See page 31.
Vernet and Delaroche. See Great Artists.
VERSCHUUR, G., *At the Antipodes,* 7s. 6d.
VIGNY, *Cinq Mars,* with etchings, 2 vols. 30s.
VINCENT, F., *Through and through the Tropics,* 10s. 6d.
—— MRS. H., *40,000 Miles over Land and Water,* 2 vols. 31s.; also 3s. 6d.
VIOLLET-LE-DUC, *Architecture,* 2 vols. 31s. 6d. each.
WAGNER. See Gr. Musicians.
WALERY, *Our Celebrities,* vol. II. part i., 30s.
WALFORD, MRS. L. B. See Low's Standard Novels.
WALL, *Tombs of the Kings of England,* 21s.
WALLACE, L., *Ben Hur,* 2s. 6d.
—— *Boyhood of Christ,* 15s.
—— See also Low's Stand. Novs.

WALLACE, R., *Rural Economy of Australia and New Zealand*, illust. 21*s.* nett.

WALLER, C. H., *Names on the Gates of Pearl*, 3*s.* 6*d.*

—— *Silver Sockets*, 6*s.*

WALTON, *Angler*, Lea and Dove edit. by R. B. Marston, with photos., 210*s.* and 105*s.*

—— *Wallet-book*, 21*s.* & 42*s.*

—— T. H., *Coal-mining*, 25*s.*

WARNER, C. D., *Their Pilgrimage*, illust. by C. S. Reinhard, 7*s.* 6*d.*

—— See also Low's Standard Novels and Low's Standard Series.

WARREN, W. F., *Paradise Found, Cradle of the Human Race*, illust. 12*s.* 6*d.*

WASHBURNE, *Recollections* (*Siege of Paris, &c.*), 2 vols. 36*s.*

WATTEAU. See Great Artists.

WEBER. See Great Musicians.

WEBSTER, *Spain*. See Foreign Countries and British Colonies.

WELLINGTON. See Bayard Series.

WELLS, H. P., *Salmon Fisherman*, 6*s.*

—— *Fly-rods* and *Tackle*, 10*s.* 6*d.*

—— J. W., *Brazil*, 2 vols. 32*s.*

WENZEL, *Chemical Products of the German Empire*, 25*s.*

West Indies. See Foreign Countries.

WESTGARTH, *Australasian Progress*, 12*s.*

WESTOBY, *Postage Stamps; a descriptive Catalogue*, 6*s.*

WHITE, RHODA E., *From Infancy to Womanhood*, 10*s.* 6*d.*

—— R. GRANT, *England without and within*, new ed. 10*s.* 6*d.*

—— *Every-day English*, 10*s.* 6*d.*

WHITE, R. GRANT, *Studies in Shakespeare*, 10*s.* 6*d.*

—— *Words and their Uses*, new edit. 5*s.*

—— W., *Our English Homer, Shakespeare and his Plays*, 6*s.*

WHITNEY, MRS. See Low's Standard Series.

WHITTIER, *St. Gregory's Guest*, 5*s.*

—— *Text and Verse for Every Day in the Year*, selections, 1*s.* 6*d.*

WHYTE, *Asia to Europe*, 12*s.*

WIKOFF, *Four Civilizations*, 6*s.*

WILKES, G., *Shakespeare*, 16*s.*

WILKIE. See Great Artists.

WILLS, *Persia as it is*, 8*s.* 6*d.*

WILSON, *Health for the People*, 7*s.* 6*d.*

WINDER, *Lost in Africa.* See Low's Standard Books.

WINSOR, J., *Columbus*, 21*s.*

—— *History of America*, 8 vols. per vol. 30*s.* and 63*s.*

WITTHAUS, *Chemistry*, 16*s.*

WOOD, *Sweden and Norway.* See Foreign Countries.

WOLLYS, *Vegetable Kingdom*, 5*s.*

WOOLSEY, *Communism and Socialism*, 7*s.* 6*d.*

—— *International Law*, 6th ed. 18*s.*

—— *Political Science*, 2 vols. 30*s.*

WOOLSON, C. FENIMORE. See Low's Standard Novels.

WORDSWORTH. See Choice Editions.

Wreck of the " Grosvenor," 6*d.*

WRIGHT, H., *Friendship of God*, 6*s.*

—— T., *Town of Cowper*, 6*s.*

WRIGLEY, *Algiers Illust.* 45*s.*

Written to Order, 6*s.*

CPSIA information can be obtained at www.ICGtesting.com
Printed in the USA
BVOW03s1738030515

398756BV00023B/224/P